Judaism Inside Out

Reclaiming the Promise of Israel

Judaism Inside Out

Reclaiming the Promise of Israel

Joshua Chasan

Water Wheel Press
Burlington, Vermont

For Ray Comstock

Contents

*O*nly a single person was created in the beginning to teach that if any individual causes a single person to perish, Scripture considers it as though an entire world has been destroyed, and if anyone saves a single person, Scripture considers it as though a whole world had been saved. Again, just a single person was created, for the sake of peace—so that no one could say to another: "My father was greater than your father;" also that the heretics could not say, "There are many ruling powers in heaven." Moreover, only a single person was created, in order to emphasize the greatness of God: for when a human being stamps many coins using one die, they are all alike; but when God stamps every individual with the die of the first person, each one of them is, nevertheless, unique. Therefore every one must say, "For my sake was the world created."

Mishnah Sanhedrin 4:5

Introduction

For almost four thousand years, the people of Israel have lived with a consciousness of humanity's potential for freedom. Other peoples have cherished the authority of conscience through which freedom is mediated. There are many ways to nurture the physical and mental capacities of human beings to live peacefully and justly with each other. Israel is one such way.

At the outset, Israel was a person, the patriarch Jacob, who had the courage to wrestle with his demons. He was called *Yisrael,* one who wrestles with his demons. Many years later, the wrestling continues. What began as Jacob's extended family has evolved into a spiritual peoplehood. A millenium ago, the philosopher/rabbi Maimonides taught that the seed of Israel is a spiritual seed, carried through the centuries by the people of Israel, who came to be called Jews when they were scattered about Earth by history.

Nowadays, most people in the world, including Jews, associate the word Israel with the nation-state created in 1948. The underlying reason for this understanding is that, after the Holocaust, leaders of the world's nations concluded that the survival of the Jews depended upon the creation of a safe haven for them. Given the nature of political and military power in the mid-twentieth century, physical security depended upon one's capacity physically to defend oneself. The people of the world, through the newly created United Nations, affirmed the restoration of independent political sovereignty for the Jewish people after almost two thousand years of political powerlessness.

The need of the Jewish people for the protection of a state persists into our own time. The continued refusal of most Arab states to recognize the State of Israel, and, more recently, the revival of anti-Semitism in many parts of the world, confirm the United Nations' judgment following World War II. Absent such independent sovereignty, the people of Israel (the Jewish people, wherever they live) would be forced back into the precariousness of existence that tempted the Nazis to try to exterminate them while most everyone else silently watched.

At the same time, the creation of the State of Israel clearly has not solved the problem of anti-Semitism. Hatred of Jews outlived the return to Jews of independent political sovereignty. Indeed, by the year 2000, traditional hatred of Jews had morphed into hatred of the State of Israel that has all the markings of historic anti-Semitism. To be sure, not all criticism of the policies and actions of the State of Israel is anti-Semitic (the freedom to criticize is a beloved right of Israeli citizens themselves). Yet, there is truth in the counsel of Dr. Martin Luther King, Jr. "My friend, I do not accuse you of deliberate anti-Semitism. I know you feel, as I do, a deep love of truth and justice and a revulsion for racism, prejudice, and discrimination. But I know you have been misled—as others have been—into thinking you can be 'anti-Zionist' and yet remain true to these heartfelt principles that you and I share. Let my words echo in the depth of your soul: When people criticize Zionism, they mean Jews—make no mistake about it."

It is easy to err in thinking about the people of Israel. From the beginning, Jews themselves have debated the significance of their own identity. Is this not essential to wrestling with God? Was not Jacob trying to find out who *he* was—not who he was in relation to his brother or mother and father; but who he himself was as a unique human being seeking to be free? If the people of Israel themselves have such difficulty in accounting for their own identity, all the more so do those who do not consider themselves a part of Israel, when they attempt to understand the Jews. In the end, the existence of the spiritual peoplehood of Israel is as much a mystery as the existence of human life; indeed, of life itself.

Now that the people of Israel have regained independent sovereignty in the historic land of Israel, it is easy to lose sight of this mystery. After all, there is nothing mysterious about struggles over boundaries of land. Early in *Genesis*, Israel encountered such difficulty. In the light of subsequent human history, there was nothing remarkable about Israel's conquest and its being conquered. In many respects, the struggle of Palestinians and Israelis today is similar to other struggles for land all over Earth. For Israel's sake and for the sake of all human beings, however, it is important that we do not lose sight of the spiritual promise of Israel that continues to wait for fulfillment. As one of humanity's historic ways of understanding its own deepest spiritual striving, the idea of Israel is not about owning land at all. It is stated in *Torah*, the heart of Israel's divine teaching, "the land belongs to God." *(Leviticus 25:23)*

The *Shoah* and the recreation of independent Jewish sovereignty are watershed events in the history of Israel, akin to the transformation of ancient Israel into rabbinical Judaism at the time of the loss of independent political sovereignty to Rome in 70 c.e. The authority of the rabbis, who assumed leadership of Israel at that time and then protected Judaism during two thousand years of wandering, is in tatters today. Just as the essence of the Temple-based religion of ancient Israel was used by the rabbis to redefine the culture of Israel, so too now the genius of the rabbis is being mined for the creation of a new stage in Israel's history. It is much too early to define the shape of Israel that is coming into being, yet this is precisely a time to reflect on the essence of Judaism.

The history of the Jews is a story of a people's challenge to understand the indivisibility of the self-interest of human beings. There is enough love in the universe for all of us to experience our stories coming true; enough food for every body to grow well. There is too much thinking that we cannot all survive. The people of Israel returned to the land of their prophets, not to fall to the lowest common denominator of conventional nationalism, but to remember the divine call at the source of who they are.

The destiny of Israel and the fate of humanity continue to be intertwined. The enduring existence of the Jews and the survival of humanity are interwoven in the mystery of the bond of human life. As it still struggles to survive physically and to remember its spiritual purpose, Israel remains an exemplar for humanity. Far more than a nation-state, Israel is a way of human living. At a time when human violence threatens life itself, Jews all over the world are called to reclaim the promise of their peoplehood: to strive always to serve divine purposes in living.

* * * *

We begin here with an assessment of the challenge to humanity at the beginning of the twenty-first century, when the genius of *homo sapiens* has brought us to the edge of our own extinction. An insight of the sages of Israel, the ancient rabbis, is offered as a way forward: the acceptance of the uniqueness and equality of every human being. The dead ends of religious and national fundamentalism are contrasted with the potential robustness of a religious pluralism that is taken seriously. We can learn to respect ourselves by embracing the spiritual dimensions of our freedom.

A spiritual nation, the people of Israel can model this kind of growth. The nature of Israel's nationality, from its personal origins in the experience of biblical figures through the shock waves of the twentieth century, is presented as background for the book's central argument. As a light unto the nations, Israel must cease relying on ethnicity as a determinant of its identity, depending instead on complete trust in the command of the eternal, holy one source of its existence. In this way, with the physical protection afforded by the State of Israel as a counter-balance to the persistence of hatred of Jews, the peoplehood of Israel can serve as a prototype for all humanity.

After the twentieth century, any religion or nation that expects a hearing must meet the test of recognizing the primacy of the unconditional love that originally called it into being. I offer this understanding of Israel to encourage other Jews to be bold and imaginative in understanding the identity of the peoplehood of Israel. As well, I hope to stimulate those who walk other spiritual paths to take the risks that we humans must take if we are to survive.

A good way to encourage such risk-taking is to tell each other our stories, to be honest about who we are and what confronts our conscience and sense of personal integrity. Such storytelling can mediate the growth of both personal and cultural freedom. We can discover that each one of us is chosen as Israel is chosen. Life as a whole is chosen. Human life is chosen to be lived in freedom. This understanding will be needed increasingly as a counterweight to the potential for tyranny posed by the new genetics. With the identification of the human genome, scientists are discovering that human characteristics that only yesterday seemed inherently personal, such as moods and dispositions of personality, are genetically determined.

Where will holiness fit into this picture of nature ruling over nurture? In what can humanity ground its freedom? Transmitted by the people of Israel, the idea of Israel comes to teach that, no matter how much of who we are is a matter of genetics, our freedom depends upon our celebrating and nurturing the part of us that has a capacity to change, to grow. The greater the reign scientists identify for nature, the more human beings are called to recognize the personal command that is the battleground for human freedom.

If we do not make the moral choices that we are called to make, the experiment on Earth of humanity and life itself may come to an end. Yet, as there is no end to space, the spiritual light that is the source of life is eternal. While we human beings are powerful enough to determine the fate of life on Earth, we are not as powerful as we want to think.

May we be as compassionate to ourselves as is the source of all existence. If we listen carefully, we can hear God telling the human story, interactively. When the music of humanity goes off key, God's pitch calls us back to harmony. You might think that we humans would be more grateful. Someday, we may be. God is rooting for us to get some humility. There is no question that it would be just what we need to hold onto whatever control is legitimately our own. God knows how hard we are tried. At this point, we need to be bold in our interpretations.

The Contemporary Situation

Unique and Equal

For thousands of years, we have struggled to recognize the value of our human differences. Only recently have we begun to transcend nasty judgments about the shape of each other's eyes and noses, the color of our skin, the ways we relate to each other sexually. We continue to struggle just to get along, one garden variety human being with another, without regard to observable physical diversity.

Our respect for each other's differences depends upon our consideration of our own distinctiveness. Our ability to see each other's uniqueness proceeds from our ability to recognize and experience our own uniqueness. As recorded by the ancient rabbis around 200 c.e. in the *Mishnah*, Israel's first legal code after the written *Torah* itself, only when each one of us is able to say with conviction, "For my sake was the world created," will we be able to recognize and accept that the universe was formed for all of us.

Of course, the sages of Israel knew how easy it is for us to take ourselves too seriously, to think that we ourselves are at the center of the world. They reminded us of our common ancestry: "Again, just a single person was created, for the sake of peace–so that no one could say to another: 'My father was greater than your father;' . . . Moreover, only a single person was created in order to emphasize the greatness of God; for when a human being stamps many coins using one die, they are all alike; but when God stamps every individual with the die of the first person, each one of them is, nevertheless, unique."

The ancient rabbis were not free of their own cultural bias. The creation of a single person in the beginning was used to defend the monotheism of Israel. "A single person was created in the beginning also that the heretics could not say, 'There are many ruling powers in heaven.'" Two thousand years later, we human beings still are only beginning to identify our cultural self-centeredness. Discovery of such wisdom comes with gratitude for human difference.

The mystery of Israel is bound up with this insight about difference. In every age, human beings ask Israel:

"Why must you be different?" And, always, Israel is called to reply:

"For my sake was the world created. As for yours."

The existence of the people of Israel comes to teach that each of us human beings is both unique and equal. It is easy for a sense of our uniqueness to get in the way of our knowing that we are equal. Today, some fear that the realization of equality will tend to lower human standards; that equality is in conflict with excellence, personal liberty and, ultimately, our freedom. They assume that equality requires sameness, just as we often associate difference with inequality and judgments of an unsavory type.

The spiritual tradition of Israel is one of a number of ways that human beings have learned to accept and embrace both the distinctiveness of each person and the inherent equality of humanity. The fullness of Israel's acceptance and embrace has evolved over time. It is challenged still by Jews whose hearts are fearful that there is not enough love to go around.

There certainly was no recognition of equality at the beginning of Israel's story about itself. In *Hebrew Scriptures*, Sarah is presented as more precious than Hagar. The birthright comes down through Isaac, rather than Ishmael; Jacob, rather than Esau (though only with Rebecca's intervention). Do such stories call into question Israel's understanding of the idea of human equality? Does Israel's idea that God chose Israel for divine service reflect its own rank ordering of human beings? Such thinking certainly is a temptation for organized religions.

Warned by both psalmists and prophets, the ancient rabbis were aware of the danger of such thinking. Though it would be foolish to read back into their words the insights of cultural anthropology and comparative religion, it is safe to say that, in their understanding of the centrality of the God of Israel to the well being of the people of Israel, the teachers of classical Judaism worshiped the God of Israel, not the people of Israel. The language of the *Mishnah* clearly reveals the ancient rabbis' sense of the centrality of the command upon each one of us to recognize his or her own uniqueness, so that each of us may be able to recognize the equality of all human uniqueness.

Every human being is equally unique. Each one of us is chosen. It is this creativity to which the story of God's promise to Abraham and Sarah points. In our day and age, this is the source of the inner strength of any spiritual tradition's capacity to pass the test of comparative religion: the understanding that one's own path to righteousness exists side by side with other ways of imagining integrity and moral viability.

The glory of our times is that, at last, we human beings are beginning to see the obvious. Being different from each other challenges us to recognize our equality. Acceptance of our equality calls us to accept the righteousness of our individuality and the uniqueness of each other. Knowing ourselves as equal and unique, we may be able to find the courage to be kind enough, to ourselves and to each other, to survive as a species.

Dangers of Fundamentalism

Fundamentalists are afraid to accept the equality of human stories. They do not realize that there truly are many ways to be lovingly kind. They fear that one's own terms of endearment are impugned by other ways of expressing love. Until religious and national fundamentalism is identified as a dead end for human growth, the life of *homo sapiens* will continue to be imperiled.

Judaism, Christianity, Islam, Hinduism are all troubled today by the judgments and actions of religious fundamentalism. Aware of the threat to life itself, people want more than the polite piety offered by mainstream religion. They look for expressions of the spirit which have the strength to speak to their uncertainties about themselves and the world. Too often, they are willing to trade in even their own freedom for what the fundamentalists say is a sure thing. In the bargain, they do not have to suffer the pangs of their own vulnerability.

It is an old game, played by leaders of state as well as of faith. Religious leaders jealously guard the boundaries of their traditions, tainting the willingness to share spiritual insights by calling it syncretism. Statecraft tends towards zero sum thinking that one's own interest is necessarily in tension with another's. States exist to protect the boundaries of their nations. As we have understood them, states fight over land rather than share it. When religious and national fundamentalism come together, any thought of sharing is throttled by the chokehold of seeing only one's own as fully human.

The understanding of fundamentalism is not limited to a few on the periphery. Majorities in ostensibly democratic societies think in gnostic terms of us and them, the good and the bad: either you are with us or against us. This is the contagion threatening party politics today, robbing it of its flexibility and resiliency. As Senator Robert Byrd reminded us in the days leading up to the Iraq War, it was Goebbels who pointed out that most masses of people, in democracies as well as in tyrannies, are vulnerable to being led one way or another.

The destiny of democracy is on the line. Democratic cultures have to be pluralistic, every point of view, every way of living given room to grow. Just as individual freedom is predicated on personal vulnerability, democracy depends upon openness to ideas, a capacity to listen carefully. The cultures of the world's democracies are now being tested.

Do people have the courage to accept and embrace both the distinctiveness of each person and the equality inherent in being human? Fundamentalism is what Erich Fromm called an escape from freedom. Fundamentalism requires only a celebration of one's own. It used to be that such tyranny left broken bodies to be buried, while survivors carried on. Now this oppression threatens life as a whole, summoning of our conscience a renewed sense of responsibility.

Our tools of communication have shrunk the world. We are given both blessing and curse. We can fall for the facade of the demagogues' false peace, beneath which we are manipulated without end; or we can find courage in the wisdom of the ages. Can we be sage enough to live in freedom?

Growing More Free

Freedom is the only legitimate goal of both religion and politics. In truth, the worlds of clergy and politicians are the same. The symbols may be different, but both seek power, the means either to control or to liberate. God and country: each conveys both the dangers of fundamentalism and a call to our better nature. Always the challenge to distinguish between what is selfish and what is of self; ever the choice before us, to be free, live freely and thrive, or to despair of being free, give up, and die.

Regardless of our politics, all of us are looking for courageous, decent leaders who recognize the ways in which so many people today are frightened. Where are the clergy and politicians who appeal to our love rather than to our fear? Regardless of our religion or our disdain for religion, we are tired of the lack of leadership from those who hide the fear and pretend it does not exist. Those who are afraid to speak the truth about the personal pain of economic injustice and a world on a war footing are not really leaders.

We human beings are tired of waiting for our story to come true. Voices of prophets still ring in our ears. We continue to wait for the time when ancient dreams of peace and freedom are fulfilled in our daily lives. We know that there always will be pain; that, being human, we have to respond to our heart's vulnerability to the contingencies of life. We hope for the day when we can distinguish clearly between pain that need not be inflicted and the normal fervor of life. We want our own tenderness accepted as the default experience in our being human.

If not yet wise, *homo sapiens* is a rather brainy specimen of life, but our mind often stops us from experiencing our own vitality, thereby limiting our expectations about how much we can share effectively with others. If we really listen, we can hear a message in our own hearts' trembling. It is a cry that comes not only from within but also from far and wide. All sentient life now feels the breath of the sun's fire as the forests are burnt and holes in the ozone widen. What is humanity doing, still carving its initials in tree trunks?

We know how to live better. We hesitate to act on our knowledge because we have accepted being bullied by the notion that we live in a tooth and claw world. The Social Darwinists never really understood Darwin. They grabbed at "survival of the fittest" to defend the cruelty of an economic competition that would benefit only a few, leaving the vast majority of human beings mired in physical deprivation. They ignored the social implications of Darwin's insight into differentiation, preferring what Stephen Jay Gould called their "mismeasure of man" to a full accounting of human uniqueness and equality.

No doubt, there is a food chain. But thousands of years ago, our ancestors recognized that, tucked within the gift of their consciousness of mind, heart and will, there was a command to live peacefully, a call to watch the universe unfold inexorably. It will continue to unfold, with or without humanity having a part in the action. The choice is ours.

One thing is for sure. We human beings can be more forgiving of each other than we want to let on. We also can be as mean as napalm. We have to step up and take control of exactly what it is that we can control. We can love the joy of justice's clarion call by helping to create moral vision. We can worship the divine love at the cutting edge of creation by being tender with each other, as we are mindful of ourselves. We know that we can be as peaceful and free as we would be. O that we already knew that we ourselves are embodied love, free to grow when we let go of the fear that we will not be respected or be unable to continue to breathe.

Renewing the Spirit

In a strange reprise of Patrick Henry's eighteenth century exhortation, "Give me liberty or give me death," we human beings now must embrace freedom as essential to who we are or we will die as a species, dramatically by our own hand, or suffocating slowly in totalitarian quicksand. We endanger our own children and grandchildren by denying the starkness of our choice.

Even as millions of us continue to starve, there is sufficient food to sustain all life on Earth. The great shame of our age, Mother Theresa observed, is our loneliness, even as there is boundless love to assure every heart of affection. If we who are *homo sapiens* truly want to survive, we must become conscious of the abundance afforded us by actively choosing to transcend our selfishness. Humanity has to learn to be obedient to the urgency of the command of its conscience.

We are not the source of our own being. That there is more to us than flesh and blood would appear to be clear to anyone who experiences emotion, yet we are tempted to reduce spiritual reality to chemistry. Life flows out of a fount that was made neither by our hands nor spun out of our imagination. God is God and human beings are God's creations. Being free requires of us a willingness to look at the arrogance in our believing that we alone are responsible for what happens. We are no more the authors of our own stories than we are the source of the food that we eat.

The better purpose of religion is to wean us of our pride by teaching us how to relate to ourselves, each other, and God. Whether one sees theology as a metaphor or a way of salvation (or both), the point of religion is not belief in God so much as our need to recognize that the great spiritual mysteries are realized in joyful relationships. The joy is not unalloyed. Human cruelty must be resisted.

God is not on any side. God does not know from sides. This is the point of God's oneness. It is the oneness of the integrity of the spiritual ground out of which we are formed. Being a universe, the universe is whole. The experience of this wholeness, *shlaymut* in Hebrew, from which comes *shalom*, is the understanding of meeting in relationship, not the contesting of sides.

Any expression of culture establishes boundaries. Just thinking, we make distinctions, establish parameters. When we act, we turn our emotions and thoughts into behavior; we associate, organize, and construct. What begins personally in a moment of inspired imagination, becomes hardened in structure that tends to get in the way of our respect and love for ourselves and for each other. It is a struggle for us to keep our minds set on freedom.

Religion and nationalism are unstable forces, as likely to explode as to be of human service. We need to be more conscious of the implications of our thinking about God and country. Increasingly, people are beginning to recognize that cultural expressions which claim to have an exclusive understanding of the truth are dangerous, no matter how inspirational their music or beautiful their buildings. The murder of Israel's Prime Minister, Yitzhak Rabin, was encouraged by rabbis. The use of passenger airliners to firebomb inhabited skyscrapers was conceived, planned, and executed by people who self-identify as religious. They did what they did in the name of their God.

The world cries out today for a bold response to the disintegrating conditions for masses of civilians now considered fair game by armed forces of nation-states and their enemies. The arrogance and violence of religious fundamentalists tempt us to reject religion in general. In the eighteenth century, advocates of the Enlightenment attacked religion for its irrationality. Many thought that reason would carry *homo sapiens* through to fulfillment of the ancient dream of a peaceable kingdom. Two hundred years later, reason itself insists that we embrace the irrational, identify with all that haunts us.

We must reclaim the ground of religious experience from fundamentalism. Religious pluralism is not the spirit watered down. It is the high way of human freedom. Accepting the integrity of the variety of spiritual stories we humans tell, we do not mitigate the integrity of each, different story. On the contrary, we release the liberating power inherent in our recognition of the interface between mutual respect and self respect. We do not need to sacrifice the true-heartedness of our own story when we accept the integrity of someone else's story that is different from our own.

Everybody is in the same boat. No living can be perfect. Not one of us can rest on his or her laurels. Integrity is not achieved once for all time. It constantly needs to be renewed by the personal moral choices that shape our lives.

Demagogues would excuse us from the messiness of our moral uncertainty by assuming for themselves all responsibility. When they say, "Follow me," they expect everybody to fall in line. They know that people can lose track of the truth. Sometimes, what is said to be real turns out not to be, and *vice versa*. Knowing a bit about spirituality, demagogues step into the vacuum. They have some sense of the mystery of how life unfolds.

When looking for a port in a storm, we are not always discriminating. Sometimes it seems that there is no difference between what is right and wrong. When people are at liberty to fudge the truth or even to lie, it gets hard to keep track of justice and injustice. We don't want to fail, so we just sign on. Like sharks smelling bloody flesh, demagogues circle around, offering illusory security in place of freedom.

The spiritual source of who we are, the source of human vitality, always needs to be renewed by our continuously struggling with our moral choices. Martin Buber pointed to a law of the entropy of holiness. It is the nature of holiness to become empty of the spirit. We replenish the spirit through the eternal revolution of our moral decision-making. Spirituality and morality are of one piece.

Mainstream religion can respond boldly if its practitioners stop undervaluing the potential of the power of religious pluralism. There is great strength in the kind of self respect that leads to mutual respect. When we are conscious of the unending necessity of our moral choices, we can recognize the danger of believing that the ultimate value of our religious tradition is its own survival. Often well hidden, this self-aggrandizement sneaks up on many decent souls who have so internalized the idea of serving their religious tradition that they confuse such devotion with serving God.

The greatest value of our religious traditions is not their survival. Any religious tradition worthy of being transmitted must allow that the value of the foundational call to unconditional love that first brought it into being trumps even the perpetuation of the tradition itself. In other words, for those who claim to be called to God-centeredness, either there is trust in God or there is not.

What happened on September 11th, 2001 was and remains for religion a call to fulfill the ancient promises of freedom and peace that are the bedrock of humanity's historic spiritual traditions. The responsibility for September 11th marking a significant change in the course of human history falls upon religious pluralism. The idea of mass murder in the name of God must be countered in the name of the spirit. The religious idea is to allow human beings to heal in every way. The experience of healing is the compassion of unconditional love. Healing is the spirit renewed through the spiritual fire that is not consumed. To heal is to be free.

Israel

BIBLICAL ROOTS

Redemption in This World

The people of Israel were commanded to tell the story of their liberation even before they left Egypt. On the very night of their departure, God told Moses and Aaron: "This day shall be to you one of remembrance: you shall celebrate it as a festival to the Eternal One throughout the ages." *(Exodus 12:14)* The ancient rabbis went further, insisting that Jews think of the Exodus every day, morning and night. "By telling the story," the *S'fat Emet*, a nineteenth century sage, explained, "we give the redemption a physical place to take hold and spread in the world." Retelling the story with words and deeds, Israel keeps alive the promise of human freedom.

Israel exists to ground humanity in a vision of its own liberation. In the flesh and blood world, only repeated effort secures a place for freedom. This is the burden of the people of Israel, shared with other human beings who understand the challenge in a variety of religious and ethical languages. In every age, the people of Israel are called to courage and an astonishing measure of trust and hope, given the sorrow of humanity's hatred and violence. The people of Israel always are asked to take the requisite risks for freedom.

By definition, Israel learns the hard way. The Hebrew word *Yisrael* means "one who grapples with God." Israel exists by accepting the fear in being human. God asks Jews to model freedom by embracing the potential of human vulnerability. God looks to the people of Israel to be exemplars in learning how to be just and live peacefully. Israel is called to accept the command, morning and night, to remember the joy of liberation.

Surviving Our Shame

Israel's story flows out of antediluvian memories of the creation, the origins of the stars, Earth and all that it contains, including us humans. The sages of Israel understood creation as an on-going process. According to *Hebrew Scriptures*, all of us animals appeared relatively late: the swarm of living creatures in the waters on the fifth day, other animals on the sixth and last day, and we human beings at its very end.

Then, right after creating humanity, God ordered the first time-out, the renewal of the seventh day of *Shabbat*. Before the sixth day ended, God deputized humanity to take care of creation, giving us the responsibility for sustaining the continuity of creation through both our own continuous labor and the renewal of *Shabbat*.

In the beginning, we felt no shame. "The two of them were naked. . . . yet they felt no shame." *(Genesis 2:25)* Only seven verses later, however, we learn that Adam and Eve were shamed by eating the fruit of the tree of knowledge. "Then the eyes of both of them were opened and they perceived that they were naked; and they sewed together fig leaves and made themselves loincloths." *(Genesis 3:7)* Loincloths suggest sexual shame, but this does not mean that the shame that they experienced was essentially sexual.

According to the sages of Israel, the ancient experience of nakedness was not physical but religious. Adam said: "I was afraid because I was naked, so I hid." *(Genesis 3:10)* Adam was afraid, the rabbis teach, because, by eating the fruit of the tree of knowledge, he stripped himself of the one commandment that he had received. He was commanded not to eat of the fruit of that tree. He ate it. Adam felt shame because he knew that when a human being loses the sense of being commanded by God, he or she truly is lost.

Is this not our situation today? Are we not ashamed of the extent to which we tend to serve ourselves rather than God and God's creation? When we are challenged to be morally responsible, we hide behind claims to moral superiority. Pity the poor ape upon whom the first human being looked down. Pity all the species disappearing in the wake of human arrogance. Instead, we pity ourselves for having to labor and being commanded to rest. It began a long time ago when our ancestors assumed that they were in control and first inflicted the pain of their selfishness. While Adam and Eve did not kill each other, their children, Cain and Abel, did not manage as well.

Yet Judaism teaches that, while justice cannot be abrogated, strict justice is tempered by a divine kindness that cannot be waived. When Cain killed Abel, God said to Cain: "What have you done? The voice of your brother's blood cries out to Me from the ground." *(Genesis 4:10)* Strict justice demanded that Abel's blood be avenged. The God of Israel, however, does not insist on strict justice. Cain was punished, but he was not killed. Even Cain, God protected. Otherwise, being human, we could not bear living. Indeed, if Cain had lost his life for killing Abel, we would not be sharing these words right now.

Abraham's Courage

The story of Israel begins two generations before the birth of Jacob, who would be called Israel for having the courage to wrestle with his demons. Abraham and Sarah were the first children of Israel, though Israel (Jacob) would be their grandchild. For all of Israel's engagement with memory, there is a non-lineal dimension to Jews' understanding of time. There is no before and after in *Torah*, God's teaching. Israel is commanded to respect the power of time, and to transcend it.

God said to Abram (whose name would become Abraham when he truly trusted in God): *"Lekh l'khah*, go forth. Leave your land, your ancestors and the house of your father." *(Genesis 12:1)* The ancient poetic ambiguity of the biblical Hebrew cries out for free-spirited interpretation. *"Lekh l'khah,"* the rabbis explain, was more than a divine order to set out on a physical journey. *"Lekh l'khah,"* God commanded Abram, go to yourself as you would go for yourself. Go for yourself as you would go to yourself. For the rabbis, there is much love in the very play of the words. Abram wanted to go for himself. He was tired of carving idols in his father's shop. At last, word had come. "Abram, you are your own person," God said. "Go for yourself. Your father will find someone else to assist him at work. Go for yourself. Fulfill the responsibilities of your own unique potential as a human being."

Abram did go forth, in so human a way. Before leaving, he took an axe to his father's idols. God knew what was going on. It would take time for this people to learn how to go for itself by going to itself, and how to go to itself by going for itself. Such an attitude depends upon an acceptance of the unfolding experience of life, an embracing of our doubts and our fears. Abram lacked the trust and sense of personal security necessary for him to fulfill the promise of Abraham. Almost four thousand years later, Israel still struggles with accepting this call.

How could Abram let in the intensity of what he was feeling, the hurt of his guilt for leaving the house of his mother and father, the ones from whose loins he physically had come? We can imagine Abram's confusion. Flushed by the rage of chopping up his father's idols, Abram struggled to absorb the wonder of God's saying, "I will make of you a great nation, I will bless you, make your name great, and you shall be a blessing." Then, strikingly, as if with no effort of his own, "Abram went." *(Genesis 12:2-4)* In a moment of time, touched by the divine, Abram opened to God's promise and heard clearly the command of his conscience.

From Abram's childhood home to the land promised by God is a distance of thousands of miles. Yet *Hebrew Scriptures* needs only five verses to move Israel's first family across Mesopotamia and then on into Canaan. Once in the promised land, Abram built a slaughter site to acknowledge his gratitude for the measure of trust and security given him. Then, we can imagine, he fell asleep and again heard God talking. Abram dreamed of his mother in her grief at his leaving. He felt his father's rage upon seeing his idols broken, realizing that it was his son who had destroyed them. Abram was not sure what his father was thinking. He knew that his mother understood that the idols were pieces of wood, carved by human hands. Yet, he knew as well, that she cherished all the love which both she and her husband invested in them. In his dream, Abram flashed back to laying his axe into the god-wood. He was ashamed. He trembled. Then the scene of the dream changed as he again felt embraced by God's blessings.

Led by God, Abram was pulled along by his own experience blazing a trail. When it was enough for him to know that God would show him where to go, Abram acted well. When he panicked at the thought that he was following the voice of an illusion, he tried to force the issue. He would tell God where to go. One day, for all of his feeling sad and alone, Abram realized that the hard part was over. When God had called, he not only had listened; he actually had heard. Like the old skin of a snake molting, a measure of his loneliness peeled away, leaving Abram free enough to be called "Abraham" by God. As time went by, Abraham began to hear more and more until, one day, he was able to resist the temptation to think that he could do whatever he chose to do, without consequence. He grew increasingly comfortable with himself and, as a consequence, was kinder, more hospitable to others. He tried to be honest and just, becoming unafraid both to serve God and, when his conscience called, to bargain with the divine voice within him.

Sarah's Laughter

We have two stories of Sarah laughing. *(Genesis 18:1-15, 21:1-7)* Each time, we know the laugh as our own. Sarah's laughter reminds us of how much we have in common with human beings who lived almost four thousand years ago. It is not difficult to imagine Sarah's laughter as our own.

The first time Sarah laughed, she was listening at the entrance of the tent she shared with her husband. It was the third day after Abraham had circumcised himself. The sun was hot and Abraham was in pain, sitting at an entrance to the tent. When three men approached, looking for refreshment, both Abraham and Sarah were eager to care for them. Then, after a hearty meal, as the men prepared to resume their journey, one of them said to Sarah:

"I will come back. Yes, I will return to you." In the words of Everett Fox's wonderful translation, "Yes, I will return to you; when time revives you will have a son." Sarah laughed within herself, the tight laughter of disbelief, edged with derision. Sarah had experienced menopause many years before. Believing that her thoughts were private, she said to herself, "*When time revives?* Now that I have withered, shall I again have delicate skin? And my husband so old."

God heard the thought behind Sarah's laughter. God said:

"Now why does Sarah laugh and say, 'Shall I really give birth, now that I am old?' Is anything beyond God? At the appointed time I will return to you, when time revives I will return and Sarah will have a son."

Sarah was scared. What was happening? Taking refuge in her fear, Sarah lied:

"No, I didn't laugh," she said.

God demands honesty, not perfection. Indeed, time revived, God remembered. Sarah gave birth to a son. No more, the laughter of doubt and derision. This time, Sarah knew the mirth of bliss. She had experienced a divine promise fulfilled in the most physical of ways, conception within her womb, a child born. On the day of Isaac's birth, it is said, many sick people were healed, many prayers answered. A lot of people were laughing with Sarah that day.

"There is no faith at first sight," wrote Rabbi Abraham Joshua Heschel in the twentieth century. "A faith that comes into being like a butterfly is ephemeral. One who is swift to believe is swift to forget. Faith does not come into being out of nothing, inadvertently, unprepared, as an unearned surprise. Faith is preceded by awe, by acts of amazement at things that we apprehend but cannot comprehend."

Faith enters our lives on the wings of our doubt. Faith comes with the love tucked inside our fear. God is kinder than we can imagine, caught up as we are in our fighting. How did Abraham and Sarah become faithful enough to the command of conscience to hear the still, small voice? In whatever time, the story is always the same. We must summon the courage to go the place that we will see only when we get there. Long before there was a physical center to Israel, a Tabernacle or Temple, Abraham and Sarah trusted in the presence of the divine sanctuary of their souls.

Torah tells us that "Sarah conceived and bore a son." This time she laughed with the mirth of a woman who knows of a visit by God. "God has brought me laughter," she said; "everyone who hears will laugh with me."

Rebecca, Esau and Jacob

Esau and Jacob, twin grandchildren of Abraham and Sarah, could not wait to be born to start fighting. According to Hebrew Scriptures, they struggled with each other in their mother Rebecca's womb. *(Genesis 25)* As the ancient rabbis told the story, Esau and Jacob were running to slay each other even as fetuses, each wanting to be the first born. Rebecca knew the pain caused by human beings thinking of life as a competition for love and for food. Rebecca bitterly complained: "If this be so, why do I exist?"

Men fighting amongst themselves has burdened women for a long time. Still, the story is about more than gender. It comes to teach the pain of human competitiveness. Anyone with a modicum of sensitivity must take note of Rebecca's grief. Yet, even Rebecca, who felt this competition within her womb, would fall into thinking of her children as combatants. After they were born, Rebecca took Jacob's side.

Each of us is different from each other, uniquely equal, equally unique. Esau was born first in a patriarchal society that favored the first-born. Savina J. Teubal conjectures that, at an earlier time, societies shaped by women favored the youngest child. Perhaps Rebecca yearned for the old order. Either way, first-born or last, birthright is understood as a matter of competition.

Almost four thousand years later, we are still trying to understand that we are not born to compete but to share. Despite the testimony of history to the contrary, life is not the zero sum game of one of us doing well only at the expense of another. We human beings are born to challenge this apprehension. Much of what we have learned about politics, economics, and society awaits revision upon the development of a new understanding of human nature.

Even more than we are subject to our physical frailty, being human we are limited in our ability to comprehend the spiritual reality of love.

Taught to share for a few years in pre-school and kindergarten, we receive opposite messages about human nature from then on. Is not an ethic of sharing as, or more, natural for *homo sapiens* than an ethic of competition? Are not reciprocity and mutual assistance necessary conditions for human well being?

We are not condemned to spill each other's blood over land, water, and food. Learning to tell our own stories with conviction, we can learn to listen to each other's stories; learn to pull together, wanting to transcend our cruelty. There are reasons for brutality being called "inhumane." We humans are still waiting to see the beauty of our own unique character. Some of us pay a fortune to reconstruct our bodies while the beauty of our souls sits within, waiting for very personal attention. No wonder we are so tempted to see each other as rivals. We are not secure of our place in this world.

Sharing our stories, we encounter ourselves and each other in all kinds of roles. Sometimes we are beauty and sometimes we are the beast; this day Jacob, another day Esau; always Rebecca. Innately, there are not good folks and bad folks. When we share our stories, we share our experiences in living. For some of what we experience, we have no responsibility. Esau was born before Jacob; Rebecca had to deal with both of them in her womb. Nobody's choices always are good ones; nonetheless do our stories unfold, challenging us to learn the morals of the tales.

Living as we do, amidst violence and greed which threaten to break social and political bonds, we definitely need the encouragement of the moral lessons. In the end, Esau and Jacob reconciled. They finally met, shared each other's stories, and were delivered of the grief they had caused themselves and each other. When we share our stories, when we learn to listen well to each other, we discover how much we have in common, and how wonderfully unique is each one of us. Through our sharing in an accounting of each other's being, we get the recognition that we crave. Sharing our stories, we identify within each other the spiritual light that also glows within us. In memory of Rebecca, may we learn to outgrow our gamesmanship before it kills us all.

Wrestling with God

> *"Your name shall no longer be Jacob, but Israel,*
> *for you have striven with beings divine and human,*
> *and have prevailed."*
>
> Genesis 32:29

What does it mean to wrestle with beings divine and human *and prevail?* Rollo May writes of the need "to identify with that which haunts you, not in order to fight it off, but to take it into your self; for it must represent some rejected element in you." Jacob prevailed. In the murky darkness of the river at night, Jacob embraced the demonic forces that threatened to tear him apart. Released from the tyranny within, he was prepared for reconciliation with his brother.

The peoplehood of Israel is founded upon Jacob's capacity to encounter all that was hidden in the shadow. To prevail in such a struggle is to embrace the demonic, to stop it from running its savage course through human history. Jacob stopped running from his fear. Terrorized by the murder of one third of its people, Israel now stands the ground of its ancient homeland. Will it stop running from its fear?

Wrestling with the demonic is not an event that is once and for all time. It is the stuff of Israel's being called to freedom. The story of Israel is one of the ways in which we humans describe the calling to freedom of *homo sapiens* as a whole.

BECOMING A PEOPLE

Go Down, Moses

"Thus saith the Lord," bold Moses said, "Let my people go!
If not, I'll smite your firstborn dead, Let my people go!"
African-American spiritual

It is hard for the slave to respond to the cruelty of the master without causing harm. The slave lives without the freedom through which the human spirit grows. The wrath of the slave knows no bounds. Slavery breeds a rage that cannot be satisfied without justice, and it is difficult to resist demands for revenge.

Who is this God of Israel? We are tempted to ask if the death of Egypt's firstborn was an act of justice or revenge? The struggle for freedom is wild. It often does not appear to make sense. After Camus, we always must strive to be neither victims nor executioners. When we fail, we have to try again. For the liberation of each one of us comes through our attitude about living and our choices about right and wrong.

Freedom is inherently optimistic. To be free, we must be hopeful that all be free. Freedom creates hope. Hope encourages us in our choices.

God tells our stories as we make our choices. Rather than asking God, "What kind of stories are you telling?" we have to engage in valuing our own moral choices. When the song of freedom plays on our heartstrings, we trust accountability to God; we must grow beyond desire for revenge. At the Passover *seder*, the people of Israel dip their fingers in the wine so that their cups do not run over. It is taught: at a time when we may be free but others are still enslaved, we mourn the loss all around. The fulcrum of the story of Israel is the indivisibility of freedom.

Israel's concern cannot be about Israel's freedom alone. Like every nation, Israel is limited by its own human perspective, but its vision defies humanity's predilection to divide itself into sides. What a Jew may hear in *New Testament* accounts of Jesus' death, an Egyptian may feel at a Passover *seder*. Human reflection on difference slides easily into the personification of good and evil. Being human, Israel is not exempt from this pride. But, like the story of humanity as a whole, Israel's story leads beyond the limits of human perspective. In its own way, Israel is asked to celebrate difference as a precondition for the growth upon which freedom rides.

Testing of Faith

The generation of the Exodus, the people who experienced first-hand the miracles in Egypt and the parting of the waters, were as easily discouraged as any of us today. While the children of Israel did take time to celebrate their freedom after walking between the walls of the sea, the singing and dancing stopped all of a sudden. In the biblical account, there is a dramatic break between Israel's rejoicing and its massive loss of hope as soon as it began to walk through the wilderness. In the end, the wandering would go on for forty years. Only two of those delivered of the sea would enter the promised land.

Immediately, there was no water to drink. *(Exodus 15:23-25)* When the former slaves did find water, it was bitter. They were dying of thirst. Where was this God who spoke to Moses, the one who had turned stick into snake, waters of the Nile into blood? Surely, one who can part a sea can manifest potable water. Three days after rejoicing that "the God of Israel reigns forever," the people of Israel despaired for their lives. Then, when they found drinkable water, they murmured because there was no food. *(Exodus 16:3)*

"If only we had died in Egypt, when we sat by the flesh pots, when we ate bread till we were satisfied. You have brought us into this wilderness to starve us to death," they accused Moses and his brother, Aaron. Within hours, quail were everywhere in their camp; manna appeared the next morning. The people were told not to gather more manna than they needed for one day. Not taking any chances, some of them scooped up as much as they could. When they awoke the next morning, the extra manna stank, infested with maggots.

The children of Israel needed time to process what had happened. Just a few days before, they had been chattel slaves. Their rejoicing at the sea was honest, their affirmation of God the sincere expression of gratitude and humility. But to die of thirst within a few days was not what they had in mind when they set out. The human heart closes quickly when throats are parched and stomachs empty.

Hatred of Israel

Not long out of Egypt, Israel was ambushed by an enmity that would appear never to subside. Hatred of Israel is as much of a mystery as Israel itself. It is the barb on the hook of Jewish history. The challenge to Israel, as to all of humanity, is to live without getting hooked.

Just out of Egypt, Israel's line of march stretched across the desert. Suddenly, Amalek's soldiers attacked Israel from the rear, killing the stragglers, the most vulnerable of the former slaves. The bitterness of the attack entered Israel's heart. *(Exodus 17:8-16, Deuteronomy 25:17-19)*

Through the ages, it would happen, again and again. From the outside, the people of Israel appeared to grow conditioned to a fear which no human being can accept without abandoning the search for freedom. Amalek "wore the signet ring of the king as Haman, the royal crown as Antiochus; the general's uniform as Titus; the emperor's toga as Hadrian; the priestly robe of Torquemada; the cossack's boots of Chmielnitzki; the brown shirt of Hitler." Rabbi Gunther Plaut's reckoning ends in the middle of the twentieth century. At the beginning of the twenty-first, we know that it still goes on.

It is Israel's call to freedom that arouses the hatred of both tyrants and those whom they oppress. More than a person, Amalek is the terror of human beings projected onto the people of Israel. God commands Israel, "You shall blot out the memory of Amalek from under heaven. Do not forget!" *(Deuteronomy 25:19)*

How to blot out the memory and not forget? The people of Israel must resist the power of memory to terrorize, while never forgetting terror's threat to freedom. Jews, too, can be Amalek. "You shall blot out the memory of Amalek from under heaven. Do not forget."

The Revelation at Sinai

The ancient rabbis told the old stories. When the people of Israel stood at Sinai, the sages of Israel said, "All grew still. No bird sang, no ox lowed, the celestial beings did not fly, the sea did not roar, no creature uttered a sound." All listened in breathless silence to the voice of eternal presence, the stillness of word at the heart of the divine. Everyone was assured of the promise of an abundance of fruit and love, the opportunity for humanity to live side by side with the other animals, secure in the embrace of God's creation.

Perhaps Moses received God's teaching word for word, both the written *Torah* of *Hebrew Scriptures*, and the oral *Torah* of the rabbis. Maybe the revelation happened in some other manner. Dictated by God to Moses, or told and retold and then written down later on, either way, the source of the stories is spiritual. As much as it may be human invention, the narrative is the response of human conscience to a divine call.

At Sinai, Israel took on new form. The extended family of Abraham and Sarah became a nation. *Torah* was the word by which the children of Israel would define the guidance of their God. The worship of Israel grew more organized, the tribe of Levi charged with the responsibilities of a well defined sacrificial rite. Beginning with Saul, a line of kings (and prophets to keep them in line) would join the Levites in leading Israel.

Over the years, memories of Sinai set in. The stillness of consciousness of the abundance of creation is one of humanity's treasures, to be shared by all. "Desist and know that I am God," King David would sing, planting the beauty of the silence of the revelation at Sinai in the hearts of all for as long as they continue to beat. *(Psalm 46:11)*

An Outsider's View

Word of Israel filtered out amongst the peoples of Canaan. Feeling threatened, the king of Moab hired a pagan soothsayer, Bilaam, to curse Israel. Reluctantly, Bilaam set forth on his ass but soon sensed a problem with his mission. When an angel of God appeared to the ass, blocking the way, the ass refused to move. Not seeing the angel, Bilaam struck the animal. After the third blow, the ass complained. God then allowed Bilaam to see the angel who then joined the ass in protesting Bilaam's cruelty, warning the soothsayer to say only what was divine. *(Numbers 22-24)*

Bilaam was commanded to bless Israel and sing its praise. In Israel's story, the God of Israel reaches out to a pagan soothsayer. A self serving invention, no doubt, but in the service of Israel's God, not the people themselves. Bilaam testified:

> *As I see them from the mountain tops,*
> *Gaze on them from the heights*
> *There is a people who dwell apart,*
> *Not reckoned among the nations.*
> *How goodly are your tents, O Jacob,*
> *Your tabernacles, O Israel!*
> (Numbers 23:9, 24:5)

"There is a people who dwell apart." The teaching from Sinai was designed to incubate Israel, to give this spiritual people its own space in which to learn to respond to God's command.

In its earliest chapters, the story of Israel is best seen in the context of other ancient stories of the origin of humanity. Such stories tend to be self-centered. There is a delightful honesty about this ancient focus on oneself. It is very human. What is striking about Israel's tale is not its focus on Israel, but the loyalty of Jews to their spiritual mission. Looking through a human lens that affords an accounting for their pride, the people of Israel tell a story that breaks the conventional national mold, even as the story is framed by its own perspective of us and them.

If it were possible for us to jettison all the old stories, write new ones from scratch, many of us would be glad to begin again. Humanity is more decent than we human beings often allege. But we cannot let go of the old stories. As a species, *homo sapiens* is commanded to remember. We have to work our way through the history, dig beneath us and them. The classical prophets of Israel point the way.

Prophetic Politics

The political standard of the prophets of Israel was radical. "Your silver has turned to dross," God chided Israel through Isaiah.

> *Your wine is cut with water,*
> *Your rulers are rogues and cronies of thieves,*
> *Every one avid for presents*
> *And greedy for gifts; they do not judge the case of the orphan,*
> *And the widow's cause never reaches them.*
>
> (Isaiah 1:22-23)

The prophets knew with a certainty that Israel's salvation depends upon its people's commitment to just living. "Zion shall be saved in judgment," Isaiah reminded the people of Israel, "her repentant ones in righteousness." *(Isaiah 1:27)*

Can any people really entrust its survival to righteousness? According to its own prophets, Israel has no choice. The prophets were not pacifists, yet they demanded the freedom and peace of universal justice. In this world broken by fear and hatred, they called the people of

Israel to cherish freedom. Freedom depends upon the peace born of the integrity of each of our souls. According to its prophets, Israel is a people who must be willing to take the risks inherent in freedom.

More than once, the people of Israel have fallen prey to losing their way, whether by ignoring the divine call at the heart of their existence, or fighting with each other, neglecting their joint survival. There are particular dangers for a nation that considers itself spiritual.

A Light to the Nations

As we have seen, the people of Israel do not appear on their own God's stage until the twelfth chapter of *Genesis.* Yet, *Hebrew Scriptures* testify that, from its early days, Israel read its story back into the origins of the world. Just as, in the beginning, God created light, Israel understood itself as called by God to be a light for all of humanity.

"Thus says the Eternal God," declared the anonymous author of Deutero-Isaiah in the sixth century b.c.e., "'I, the Eternal, have called you in righteousness, and taken you by the hand. I am the One who created you and made you a covenant people, a light to the nations: to open eyes that are blind, to bring the captives out of confinement, those who sit in darkness, out of the dungeon.'" *(Isaiah 42:1,6,7)*

Israel was called to be apart from the other nations in order to teach humanity about the spiritual light of its freedom. There were times, of course, when Israel betrayed the essence of this call by actively seeking to impose its story on other nations. In the cherished prayer of the synagogue service, *Alenu (It is Incumbent Upon Us),* with which Jews have concluded worship for centuries, Israel looks to the time when "all who dwell on earth" will "recognize that every knee must bend and every mouth swear allegiance" to the God of Israel. No doubt, many Jews have understood these words in a triumphal sense. Tradition attributes the prayer to Joshua, in whose time the people of Israel, by force of arms, took possession of the land promised to Abraham and Sarah.

There is nothing unique about one nation's dispossession of another. In settling the Americas, Europeans virtually exterminated the native nations, a process that continued in Central and South America even after the world struggled to absorb what had happened in Europe during World War II. Violent assaults of human beings on each other have a long history.

That the stories of human beings are open to interpretation is cause for both delight and concern. It is through flights of imagination that humanity practices both being free and robbing humanity of its freedom. If they want, those who fear and hate Israel today can read the biblical account of Joshua's conquest of ancient Canaan into their understanding of the creation of the State of Israel after the Holocaust. Isaiah's description of Israel as a light unto the nations can be interpreted as typical of any nation's self-aggrandizing claims. Notwithstanding the allegations of Jew-haters, Jews *are* human beings, caught up by the same historical forces as everyone else.

Yet, precisely because of Deutero-Isaiah's notion that God charged the people of Israel to be a light to the nations, each generation of Jews for millennia has heard a warning against descending to the lowest common denominators of human behavior. "You are my witnesses," God said through Deutero-Isaiah, "My servant whom I have chosen. Know me, therefore, and put your trust in me; understand that I am the one. Before me no god was formed and after me none shall be. Be sure that I am the eternal God, and I alone can deliver you." *(Isaiah 43:10-11)*

This is the traditional bedrock of Israel's story. It was read by Deutero-Isaiah into the creation story at the beginning of *Torah*, and it is found at the end of *Torah*. Just before his death, Moses reminded the people of the spiritual ground upon which they were commanded by God to stand as they entered the promised land:

> *The Rock! God's work is perfect:*
> *For all God's ways are justice;*
> *A God of truth and without iniquity,*
> *Just and right is God.*
>   (Deuteronomy 32:4)

"For all God's ways are justice." It was baffling to the former slaves who began the forty years of wandering in the wilderness. No doubt, it was baffling to the next generation as it prepared to enter the new land. It is baffling still. Nonetheless is it Israel's truth. The rock of God is alive to the consciousness of the people of Israel inasmuch as they remember the essence of their story. In Moses' words, the source of the animating force of the spirit of Israel is the incomparable wholeness of "the Rock that begot you…the God who brought you forth." *(Deuteronomy 32:18)* Again and again, the refrain: Israel must trust in God. While King David certainly did not always live up to this standard, he gave it eloquent expression:

> *Trust in the Eternal One and do good;*
> *Dwell in the land and be nourished by faith . . .*
> *And God will bring forth as the light your righteousness*
> *and your judgment as the noonday.*
>
> (Psalm 37:3,6)

The prophets of Israel transformed this faith into a moral vision for all of humanity. In Rabbi Heschel's words, "[w]hat concerns the prophet is the human event as a divine experience."

> *For behold, the Eternal One shall go forth from the*
> *place of the divine*
> *To punish the iniquity of the inhabitants of Earth,*
> *And Earth shall disclose the blood shed upon her,*
> *And shall no longer cover up her slain.*
>
> (Isaiah 26:21)

Who Israel is, why Israel survives, what Israel must be about if the people of Israel are to be secure, are all dependent upon Israel's trust in the original and continuing source of its existence. According to its own story, as long as Israel offers up the fuel of such trust, feeding the spiritual fire at its core, the people of Israel can depend upon the redeeming power of Israel's God. Trusting God, Israel is faithful to the continuity of its peoplehood and shares in the divine light with all of humanity. Israel is God's witness to the spiritual truth that makes flesh and blood so precious. The ancient rabbis went so far as to imagine God as saying to Israel: "If you are not my witnesses, as it were, I would not be God."

Malachi's Esau

Israel is tempted to take itself too seriously. Being God's partner has its opportunities and its temptations. Over the course of centuries, the behavior of the people of Israel evoked constant reminders from prophets, such as Micah, who asked: "What does the Eternal One require of you but to do justice, and to love kindness, and to walk humbly with your God." *(Micah 6:8)*

When God instructed Isaiah that "My house shall be a house of prayer for all people," *(Isaiah 56:7)* the ultimate hope was not that Israel would force everyone to worship its God in its Temple. The prophets of Israel looked toward the time when justice would "roll down like waters, and righteousness like a mighty stream." *(Amos 5:24)*

> *Learn not the way of the nations,*
> *Nor be dismayed at the signs of the heavens*
> *Because the nations are dismayed at them,*
> *For the customs of the nations are false.*
> (Jeremiah 10:2,3)

A world was possible in which the lion would lie down with the lamb. Israel was to lead the way.

There was great temptation for Israel to think itself better than others. After all, Jews are human beings, and human beings tend to be self-centered. The human eye wanders; our appetites often get the best of us. God's great claim on the standard of behavior of the people of Israel often seemed to trap them between the rock of great expectation and the hard place of ordinary, human weakness. Though they universalized the mission of Israel, expanded its national purpose to include the fulfillment of the promise of justice and peace for humanity as a whole, the prophets themselves were human beings of their own time and place.

In the fifth century b.c.e., an anonymous prophet known to us only as Malachi ("My messenger") retold the story of Esau and Jacob with a twist. As it appears in the written *Torah*, Esau and Jacob jockeyed for position in their mother Rebecca's womb. When they were born, Jacob was called Jacob because he had grabbed at Esau's heal as his brother was being born first. Their mother Rebecca managed to negate the order of birth. Allowing Jacob to benefit from the rights of the first born, she helped to fulfill the biblical prophesy that "two separate peoples shall issue from your body; one people shall be mightier than the other, and the older shall serve the younger." *(Genesis 25:23)*

As the boys grew up, we learn from *Torah*, Esau became a hunter, while Jacob was a quiet man. The narrative of the story makes it clear that history was on Jacob's side, though he took advantage of his brother and deceived his father. At his worst, Esau appears rash, boorish, and clumsy. In the end, however, the account in *Torah* crescendos to a dramatic reconciliation, not only of the two brothers, but also of Jacob and his children as well.

When Malachi retold the story of Jacob and Esau in the middle of the fifth century b.c.e., Judea was a Persian province and the prophet was speaking to the social and religious issues of his day. *(Malachi 1:1-3)*

According to Rabbi Gunther Plaut, it was a time when "[p]eople doubted God and divine justice; their Temple service was perfunctory." There was confusion about the nature of Jewish identity and a generalized sense of not knowing where things were going.

What did Malachi hear God telling him to instruct the people of Israel? "I have loved you, says the Eternal One. But you say: 'How have You shown Your love for us?' God says: Was not Esau Jacob's brother... and yet I loved Jacob?" The inference is that God did not love Esau. In fact, it is not left to inference at all. Malachi continues: "I have loved Jacob, but Esau I have hated, and laid his mountains waste, and made his inheritance into a lamentation for a wilderness." In retelling the story of Jacob and Esau, Malachi put a spin on it. Where does it say in *Genesis* that God hated Esau? It does not. Malachi echoed Rebecca's favoring of Jacob, turning it even harsher than in the biblical story.

Malachi is the last of the prophetic books of Hebrew Scriptures. After Malachi, according to those who then began to tell and shape the story of Israel (first the *sofrim*, the scribes, and then the sages of Israel, the ancient rabbis), God may have continued to speak to individuals, but the message was not intended for the community at large. Such judgments were to be made only by those who were well versed in the tradition, the rabbis themselves. As this change appeared on the horizon, the last of the classical prophets of Israel bore witness to the limits of even prophetic vision.

By this time, the children of Israel had suffered the radical dislocations of the destruction of Solomon's Temple, loss of sovereignty in their own land, and exile to Babylonia. With the Persians' defeat of the Babylonians, some of the exiles returned and built the Second Temple, but the old Temple rite was practiced without enthusiasm. Members of the priesthood were not always faithful to their duties. The Jewish people were not particularly interested in the old stories.

More than one commentator has said that the Temple was rebuilt but under-funded. God sent Malachi to reawaken the spirit of the people. How did this prophet do it? In the old, classical way of *homo sapiens,* by dividing humanity into the two groups with which we continue to be familiar, us and them. According to Malachi, God loves us, descendants of Jacob; God hates them, descendants of Esau. After all, Esau historically was associated with Edom, and Edom with Rome; and it was Rome that destroyed the Holy Temple the second time, sending Israel into its long exile.

Listen to Rabbi Samson Raphael Hirsch, living in nineteenth century Germany, describe the character of Esau-Edom: "The principle of Esau-Edom is the worship of force, the laurel of blood is its highest ornament, plans for conquest of the world form the dream of the greatest of its world-historic great ones." For Rabbi Hirsch, "this Esau-principle is in complete contrast to the Divine order of the world that fixes the rule of justice and right and love on the foundation of the sanctification of life as the highest, as the sole goal. In the service of this highest human goal the principle of the life of Jacob stands, in contrast to that of Esau-Edom. The Esau-principle is what God hates, the Jacob-principle what God loves."

One can, of course, take the Jacob principle and the Esau principle as inclinations within each one of us. But Malachi's words echo strongly: God loved Jacob. God hated Esau. For a very long time, we human beings have tended to think of Jacob and Esau as personifying "us" and "them," despite the fact that this notion that God hated Esau is not supported by the story as told in *Genesis*.

It is true that, according to *Torah*, the story of the Jewish people comes down through Jacob. We do not give this truth justice, however, when we think of God loving Jacob and hating Esau. Indeed, earlier in the nineteenth century than Rabbi Hirsch, the Chasidic master, Rabbi Menahem Mendel of Kotzk understood Esau as looking pretty much like Jacob: "Esau was no clumsy peasant dressed in fancy garments who walked around barefoot and tended his pigs. Esau had a long beard and *peyos* (side locks). He was the leader of a great clan, who would recite *Torah* carefully."

What was the Kotzker suggesting? Could it be that Jacob and Esau do represent inclinations within each of us? Elsewhere, the Kotzker teaches: "Not only is one who hates another soul called wicked–but someone who hates himself is also called wicked." When we project the hatred, whether onto ourselves or others, we change the story. It was easy enough for Jacob to deceive Esau. It is even easier for us to deceive ourselves.

SUSTAINING THE VISION

The Rabbinical Reform

The spiritual tradition of Israel began as the religion of the ancient Israelites. It was founded in the experiences of the patriarchs and matriarchs, defined by the revelation at Mount Sinai, and developed by kings and prophets. Then, within the same context of Greco-Roman culture and Roman rule out of which Christianity emerged, came a big change. The priests and Levites of the Temple, the monarchy and its nemesis, prophecy, all gave way to the rabbis.

Already by the time some of the exiles had returned from Babylonia (around 500 b.c.e), people realized that the old glory of Israel would not be restored. Old people, who had seen the wonder of King Solomon's Temple as children, wept in the streets of Jerusalem at the sight of the new one. Israel's kings ruled at the behest of one imperial power or another until sovereignty was lost completely in 70 c.e. Especially after the descendants of the Maccabees (Chanukah's heroes) took control of state and the Holy Temple in the second century b.c.e., it became clearer that revolutionary change was in order. Nationalist zealots thought that the rule of Rome could be overthrown by armed resistance. They failed. Gradually, the people of Israel would wake to the leadership of the rabbis, whose approach to Israel's challenges was founded in lessons learned from the destruction of Solomon's Temple and exile to Babylonia.

With the return from exile, Ezra, a priest who also was a scribe, assumed leadership of Israel. The exiles in Babylonia had managed to keep their identity in tact far more than did those Israelites who had remained in the land of Israel where they intermarried in great numbers. Ezra summoned the people to a meeting at which he sounded an alarm about the fate of Israel. At this same meeting, he announced the banishment of the non-Israelite members of intermarried families. *(Ezra 10)*

Ethnicity always was a factor in defining the identity of Israel. God's original promise to Abraham and Sarah was that their seed would found a large nation. In biblical days, one born of an Israelite father was bound to be an Israelite. At the same time, in those early days, what we would now speak of as existential identity was a factor in transmitting the tradition. Isaac was an Israelite as much for how he lived, how he saw himself in relationship with the God of Israel, as for being the son of Abraham. Likewise, Abraham circumcised not only himself and his sons, but all the members of his household, whether or not they were related by blood.

After the Babylonian Captivity, Ezra boldly banished both "the alien women of the peoples of the land" who had married Israelites, and their children. *(Ezra 10:2,3)* The exile to Babylonia had shocked Israel. When the exiles returned, they labored to rebuild the Temple and reestablish the sacrificial rites, but a measure of confidence in the mission of the Temple cult was lost. With the *mizbeah* (altar) of the Temple despoiled, destroyed, there was a great need for order. The light of the *menorah* was extinguished. Would the light in the souls of the people of Israel continue to shine?

For reasons still very much debated, it was during Second Temple times that Israel's standard of ethnic identity changed from patrilineal to matrilineal. Perhaps it was a matter of knowing better the identity of a mother than a father at a time when the people of Israel began to develop a consciousness of their dispersion. Perhaps it was the influence of Roman law. For whatever reason, there was a power to the synergy between the standard of matrilineality and Ezra's concerns about ethnic integrity.

No longer assured of home in *Eretz Yisrael* (the land of Israel), Israel decentralized, basing itself in a meeting house called a *bayt midrash*, literally a house of interpretation, of study. The synagogue became the community center of Israel, the place where people prayed, studied, and met for a variety of other purposes. The religious culture of Israel grew within the *bayt midrash*. The ancient tradition of Israel evolved into what came to be known as Judaism. Dispersion took the place of geographic integrity.

Abiding still was the old spiritual core of Israel, its covenantal relationship with God. As the modern Israeli historian Yehezkel Kaufmann writes of that time, "Israel has not abandoned its God, and God has not abandoned Israel. The covenant is eternal, and in it is the assurance of the glory of Israel in the time to come."

Ezra renewed the covenant entered into by Abraham and Sarah and nationalized at Sinai. Before the assembled people in the streets of Jerusalem, Ezra not only sent away the foreign born; he read from a scroll that historians believe was an early form of the written *Torah*. Ezra introduced to Israel what would become the central ritual of the synagogue service, regular study of traditions once oral and increasingly scribed on parchment. Through the following twenty-five hundred years, the power of Israel's traditional spirituality continued to grow within a variety of ethnic cultures around the world, creating what came to be known as Judaism.

The Second Commonwealth of Israel lasted about half a millennium, an interregnum between ancient Israel and rabbinically defined Judaism. There was great substance to the culture of Israel through these centuries. Books were written that would become part of the canon of *Hebrew Scriptures* when it was organized later by the rabbis. Between 500 b.c.e. and 70 c.e., many ideas and practices that the ancient rabbis would ordain as tradition had an opportunity to germinate. Scholars and teachers began to translate the ideas of biblical Israel from the old language of the Temple and its sacrificial cult into forms of study of written and oral traditions that would become *halakhah*, literally, the way of Judaism. The synagogue became a local place where these traditions could be endlessly debated, creating over time the links of the chain of tradition *(masorah)*.

The political situation in the larger world was difficult, to say the least. It was only a matter of time before the string of vassal kings and corrupt priests would lose the last of their authority. In 70 c.e., the Romans sacked Jerusalem and left desolate the sacred place of the Temple. It was time for the rabbis to step fully out of the shadow of the Second Temple and assert their leadership. The change is memorialized in the story of Rabban Yohanan ben Zakkai, walking with his disciple, Rabbi Joshua, near the ruins of Jerusalem:

"Rabbi Joshua looked at the destruction and said:

'Alas for us! The place which atoned for the sins of the people Israel through the ritual of animal sacrifice lies in ruins!' Then Rabban Yohanan ben Zakkai spoke to him these words of comfort:

'Be not grieved, my son. There is another way of gaining atonement, through deeds of loving kindness.' For it is written, 'Loving kindness I desire, not sacrifice.'" *(Hosea 6:6)* Literally, the Hebrew words for loving kindness, *gemilut hasadim*, have the sense of dealing fully with God's redeeming love. *Gemilut hasadim* consists of experiences of the reciprocity of love. In the absence of the sacrificial rite, atonement was to be attained through loving relationship.

Rabban Yohanan ben Zakkai was well known for his courage and wisdom. There were many rabbis then, people whose learning and concern for public and private integrity, earned them the loyalty of the people of Israel. We have the sermon of one of these teachers, his name forgotten, who called Israel back to its own inner strength amidst the desolation that the Roman army left in its wake. "We are not led by flesh and blood rulers," this rabbi reminded the survivors of the war with Rome. "We are led by the spirit of God. When the children of Israel came through the parted waters, they sang, *'Mi khamocha ba'aylim ha'shem, Who among the mighty compares with you, Eternal One?'* That's why, morning and night, we are taught to sing the words that were sung by the ones who walked through the parted waters: *'Who is like you, O Eternal One?'*

"Beware of comparing God with a flesh and blood ruler," the preacher insisted in the face of the all too real evidence of the destructive power of flesh and blood rulers. "Mortal rulers expect their subjects to run before them, clearing the way. The emperor of Rome expects us to spread carpets at his feet so that they do not touch the ground. The emperor expects pillows to lean on, sumptuous meals to taste. He wants bright torches to light his way at night.

"But our God is very different from the emperor of Rome. Our God does not insist upon our loyal service as a precondition for being good to us. Our God does the very opposite. We can depend upon our God to make the first move. We are born into a world that is clothed by God. God clothes the fields with grass so that our footsteps may be gentle. God lights the world with the sun and the moon, prepares the widest variety of foods.

"God doesn't wait for us to adorn God's place. God adorns God's place with mountains and lakes. The flowers bud for us, and birds sing. God's dominion is without end. This is why the children of Israel sang, *'Ha'shem yimlok l'olam va'ed, the reign of the Eternal One is forever.'*"

The ancient rabbis knew the burden that was upon them. They were worldly men, many of whom were conversant with the Greco-Roman culture of their time. When they looked to find a new way to honor the memory of the exodus from Egypt (remembering was a command upon Israel even before leaving their slave quarters), they chose the form of the Greek *symposium*, a celebratory meal at which participants imbibed four cups of wine and engaged in the give and take of raising questions and considering answers. As Rabbi Barukh Bokser has described, the origins of the form of the Passover *seder* were pagan!

The ancient rabbis knew how important it was for Israel to retain an understanding of the timelessness of its reason for being. The sages of Israel loved to play with the stories of Israel. Though they lived a long time after all had grown still at Sinai, they remembered their ancestors' experience at Sinai as if it had happened in their own time. They were in awe of the stories which they had inherited, and they were not afraid to play with them. Their love of *talmud Torah*, the shared learning of ancient stories and traditions, was robust and unfettered by concern that they were overstepping their bounds with their wildly imaginative interpretations. The ancient rabbis were confident enough in their cultural sophistication to play with the traditions with the naive wonder of children. With political skill and *yirat ha'Shem* (awe of God), they led Israel through a revolution that would ensure the survival of its call to freedom for the next two thousand years. The sages of Israel taught the play of learning.

Playing With Time

The ancient rabbis loved the play of learning. They played with words and letters, with interpretations both serious and funny. They played with time itself. For example, when Moses reached heaven, where he was to receive the *Torah*, he found God busy decorating the letters of the *Torah* with elaborate crowns (which, to this day, can be found on the hand-crafted letters of each *Torah* scroll). Moses stood there, amazed. God said to him:

"Don't you know how to say 'shalom?'" Moses replied:

"Should a servant greet his master first?" God said:

"You might at least have wished Me success in my work!"

"May you succeed in all Your works," Moses said, then stared at the beautiful ornaments with which God decorated the letters of *Torah*. He asked God what they meant. God told him:

"In later years there shall live a man named Akiba, son of Joseph, who will fashion a mountain of interpretations and laws based on every dot crowning these letters." Moses said:

"Show me this man!" So God transported Moses to Rabbi Akiva's classroom and Moses took a seat on one of the back benches from where he listened to the master and his students discussing *Torah*. Moses was ashamed of his ignorance. He could not follow a word that was spoken. Then he heard one of the students asking Rabbi Akiba:

"Master, how do you know that this is so?" Rabbi Akiba answered:

"This is a tradition given to Moses on Mount Sinai." It pleased Moses to hear such wisdom credited to him, even though he himself did not understand it.

"Surely this is a great teacher!" he thought to himself.

When Moses returned to heaven from his visit to Rabbi Akiba's school, he asked God:

"Why do You give the *Torah* to Israel through me when You have such a teacher as this in Your world?" God wanted to encourage his prophet:

"Relax, Moses, I know what I'm doing. Pay attention to what I want you to do." Moses then asked God:

"Now that I have seen this man's great learning, may I also see his reward?" God said:

"Turn around and look." So Moses turned around and saw a great amphitheater filled with people. There in the center stood an old Rabbi Akiba, surrounded by Roman soldiers who were raking his flesh with sharp iron combs, until he died.

"Is this the reward for such great learning?" Moses cried out. God answered:

"Moses, I share your grief. Such cruelty is not the intention of my gift of freedom to humans. Tragically, over the years this cruelty will continue. May human beings learn to be responsible with their freedom."

At that moment in heaven, Moses was approached by one of Rabbi Akiba's teachers, affectionately known as Nahum Gam Zo. Actually, his name was Nahum and he was from a place called Gimzo. The people called him Nahum Gam Zo because he always was saying, *"gam zo l'tovah,* this too is for the good."

Nahum Gam Zo had a great influence on Rabbi Akiba. As Nahum was known for saying "this too is for the good," Rabbi Akiba was known for his expression, "It is always good to say, 'Everything God does is for the best." Nahum Gam Zo wanted to comfort Moses, to get his mind away from painful thoughts about the cruelty of Rabbi Akiba's death. He sought to remind him of Akiba's courage, not only in dying but also in living. So Nahum told Moses another story about Rabbi Akiba:

Once Rabbi Akiba went out walking and he came to a town. He wanted to stay there for the night, but they wouldn't give him lodgings. He said:

"Everything God does is for the best." Then he went out to a field where he slept overnight. He had with him a candle, a rooster, and a donkey. During the night, the wind blew out the candle, a cat came and ate the rooster, and a lion came and ate the donkey. When Akiba awoke, he said:

"Everything God does is for the best." That same night an army had passed by where Akiba was sleeping, had captured the town, and killed most of the inhabitants.

"How right I was to say that everything God does is for the best!" Akiba said to himself. "For had they let me stay in town, I would surely have been killed. And had my candle been lit or the rooster crowed or the donkey brayed when the army came through, that too would have brought about my end."

Moses had listened carefully to Nahum's story about Akiba. He let it sink in. Then he said to Nahum:

"Had Akiba died that night simply of a sword, he would not have had to endure such a painful death at the hands of the Romans." At this point, Akiba himself overheard the conversation. He reminded Moses:

"Everything God does is for the best. Life is paradoxical. God foresees everything and we humans have the freedom to make our own choices. There are difficulties, pain in each of our lives. But there need not be as much pain as we inflict on ourselves and each other."

Authority of the Rabbis

Though many of the ancient rabbis shared in the spiritual gifts of Rabbi Akiva, they did not think that the source of their authority was a direct line to God. A story from the *Babylonian Talmud* reveals the very human way, through the gift of their play, that the sages of Israel not only justified their leadership, but also transformed the search for freedom of biblical Israel into the rabbinic trust in the freedom of the interplay between cognitive learning and the pursuit of deeds of loving kindness.

"It has been taught: On that day, Rabbi Eliezer brought forward all the arguments in the world, but the other sages did not accept them. Rabbi Eliezer then said to them:

'If the *halakhah* agrees with me, let this carob-tree prove it!' (Literally "the way," *halakhah* is more commonly understood to be the norms and laws of rabbinical Judaism.) At that moment, the carob-tree was torn a hundred cubits out of its place—others say, four hundred cubits.

'No proof can be brought from a carob-tree,' the sages responded. Again, Rabbi Eliezer said to them:

'If the *halakhah* agrees with me, let the stream of water prove it.'
The stream of water flowed backwards.'

'No proof can be brought from a stream of water,' the sages said.
Again, Rabbi Eliezer said:

'If the *halakhah* agrees with me, let the walls of the schoolhouse
prove it,' at which point the walls inclined to fall. But Rabbi Joshua
rebuked the walls, saying:

'When scholars are engaged in a dispute about *halakhah*, why are
you interfering?' As a consequence, the walls did not fall, in honor of
Rabbi Joshua, nor did they resume the upright position, in honor of
Rabbi Eliezer, and they are still standing thus inclined. Again, Rabbi
Eliezer said to the other sages:

'If the *halakhah* agrees with me, let it be proved from Heaven!' At
that moment, a Heavenly Voice cried out:

'Why do you dispute with Rabbi Eliezer, seeing that in all matters,
the *halakhah* agrees with him!' But Rabbi Joshua then stood up and
said, citing words from *Torah*:

'It is not in heaven.' " *(Deut. 30:12)*

The *Talmud* itself then asks:

"What did Rabbi Joshua mean by citing these words?' " And the
Talmud offers a response from Rabbi Jeremiah:

"Rabbi Joshua was saying that the *Torah* already had been given at
Mount Sinai. Therefore, we pay no attention to a Heavenly Voice,
because You long ago wrote in the *Torah* at Mount Sinai: 'After the
majority one must incline.' *(Exodus 23:2)*

"Later, in Heaven, Rabbi Nathan met the prophet Elijah and asked
him: 'What did the Holy One, blessed be, do in that hour?' Elijah said:
'God laughed with joy, saying, 'My children have defeated Me, My children have defeated Me.' "

If the other sages had doubted Rabbi Eliezer's spiritual gifts, he certainly demonstrated them. But Rabbi Joshua spoke for all of his rabbinical colleagues when he quoted from *Deuteronomy*: "It is not in
Heaven," meaning, since the *Torah* was already given at Mount Sinai,
there no longer was a need to listen to Heavenly Voices. Rather, as supported by a verse from *Exodus*: "After the majority one must incline."

The story depends upon two proof texts, both of which the sages
of the *Talmud* turned on their heads to make the point that they wanted to make about rabbinical authority. It was fully within the bounds
of rabbinic discourse for these sages to interpret these verses as they did,
but the measure of their boldness in establishing their own authority is

underlined by the meaning of these verses in their original contexts.

Rabbi Joshua justified the sages ignoring the Heavenly Voice heard by Rabbi Eliezer by citing a few words from one of Moses' orations at the end of *Torah*. Moses had sought to reassure the people that being faithful to the covenant would not be a difficult task. He said:

"Surely, this commandment which I enjoin upon you this day is not too baffling for you, nor is it beyond reach. *It is not in the heavens,* that you should say, 'Who among us can go up to the heavens and get it for us and impart it to us, that we may observe it?' Neither is it beyond the sea, that you should say, 'Who among us can cross to the other side of the sea and get it for us and impart it to us, that we may do it?' No, the word is very close to you, in your mouth and in your heart, to do it." *(Deuteronomy 30:11-14)*

The plain meaning of "It is not in the heavens" is that the word of God is as close to Israel as one's own mouth or heart. In their original context, the words make a wonderful proof text for an understanding of a direct relationship between the people of Israel and their God. The sages of the *Talmud,* however, wanted to teach a very different lesson: that, because *Torah* already was given at Mount Sinai, "It is not in the heavens," and therefore Rabbi Eliezer's special connection to the divine was not relevant. What counted was the opinion of the majority of the sages, as it is said: "After the majority, one must incline." *(Exodus 23:2)*

The verse from *Exodus* is one rule amongst many that appear in *Torah* immediately after the description of the revelation of the Ten Commandments. According to the New Jewish Publication Society translation, the complete statement (verses 2 and 3) reads: "You shall neither side with the mighty to do wrong–you shall not give perverse testimony in a dispute so as to pervert it in favor of the mighty–nor shall you show deference to a poor man in his dispute." Following the line of thought of the traditional rabbinic interpretation found in the story in the *Talmud,* the Stone Edition of the *Torah* offers: "Do not be a follower of the majority for evil; and do not respond to a grievance by yielding to the majority to pervert [the law]. Do not glorify a destitute person in his grievance."

The editors of the Conservative Movement's *Etz Hayim, Torah and Commentary* point out that the word translated by the Jewish Publication Society as "mighty" was traditionally understood as "majority," and this verse was used by rabbinical courts as support for their abiding by the majority of the rabbis. Yet, the editors also state that, in all likelihood, the verse "expresses a warning not to pervert justice by deferring to the majority view if one is convinced that it is erroneous." Clearly, the ancient rabbis turned the verse on its head to justify following a majority of the members of their own courts.

Boldly and without apology, the sages of Israel placed themselves between God and the Jewish people. They stepped in at a time when the ability of the people of Israel to fulfill its historic calling was challenged by its loss of the traditional tools to do so, the Holy Temple and independent sovereignty in the land of Israel. The rabbis rescued Israel when the people again were forced to wander, this time not in the desert for forty years, but throughout the world for almost two thousand. The rabbis' fertile minds and their love for the people of Israel enabled Israel to secure its relationship with God when the divine promise of Israel's greatness in Canaan was beginning to seem like a completed chapter in history.

The rabbis were careful to link their claim to authority to the biblical tradition. The first teaching of *Pirkei Avot (Sayings of the Fathers)*, historically the most popular tractate of rabbinic literature, establishes a direct connection between God's giving the *Torah* at Sinai and the rabbis themselves:

Moses received the Torah from Sinai and transmitted it to Joshua, Joshua to the Elders, the Elders to the Prophets, and the Prophets to the Men of the Great Assembly. They said three things: be patient in judgment; raise up many students; and make a fence for the Torah. (Pirkei Avot 1:1)

The history of the Great Assembly remains clouded by time. We know that the rabbis regarded Ezra as its leader, and they attributed the origins of such basic building blocks of Judaism as *halakhah* (law) and *aggadah* (legend) to the Great Assembly. Making "a fence for the Torah" came to be seen as a way to create a shield of rabbinical ordinances to protect the sanctity of the inner core of the tradition. For example, one does not sound the *shofar* when *Rosh Hashanah* falls on *Shabbat*, for fear that one would violate *Shabbat* restrictions on carrying through a public domain.

More than two thousand years later, however, in the nineteenth century, Rabbi Joshua Heschel of Monstritch offered an idiosyncratic reading about creating a fence around the *Torah*. It is an interpretation that works well for Jews of our time. Great patience was needed, said Rabbi Joshua Heschel, "for Israel's journey would not be easy." Good teaching was required "so that many people would remain loyal to God's *Torah*." And, departing completely from conventional interpretation, Rabbi Joshua Heschel held that Israel was to create a fence around

Torah "through loving acceptance of the harshness of the tribulations of the exile."

Clearly, Rabbi Joshua Heschel allowed himself great latitude in his thinking. Yet, we must remember that it was the rabbis' insistence on freedom for their imagination that gave Judaism its strength and staying power. As a form of exegesis, rabbinical *midrash* (interpretation) continues to be a vital way of teaching because the intellectual freedom it encourages is a direct descendent of the ancient call of freedom to Israel to be heard in *Hebrew Scriptures*.

The problem for the rabbis of our own time is that most Jews no longer accept traditional rabbinic explanations for the harshness of Israel's tribulations. A combination of the Enlightenment's faith in reason, the barbarity of the *Shoah*, and the founding of the State of Israel, eroded most Jews' willingness to rely on rabbinical judgments to shape their lives. The revival of *talmud Torah* in our time testifies to the creativity of Israel's teachers for the past two thousand years, but it does not gainsay that most Jews in the twenty-first century rely on their own conscience or a direct relationship with God, rather than rabbinical interpretation of *halakhah*.

Like the Levites before them, whose beautiful song helped to create the Temple's special place of sanctity, the rabbis stepped into the history of Israel with the grace of God. Their evolving understanding of Israel's needs allowed for the creation of rabbinical Judaism, which now forms, along with the spiritual tradition of biblical times, the bedrock of the culture of Israel. As long as there are people of Israel, they will study the sacred texts of Israel's sages. For purposes of judging right from wrong, however, after the *Shoah*, the people of Israel once again stand in direct relationship with their God.

Hard Questions

After the Shoah

The Nazis bequeathed to all humanity an unprecedented acceptance of murder and genocide. The damage did not end with their defeat. The Nazis raised the threshold of pain that human beings abide as nation-states clash with each other. The Allies themselves were not exempt from attacks on innocent civilian populations. We realize now that none of us can afford to await the worst, believing that we will be spared. The longer we stand by, the deeper the poison of complacency seeps into our souls.

Astonishingly, even the *Shoah* did not rip from Israel's heart its people's loyalty to God. Through the 1940s, there remained Jews who affirmed the confidence of Israel's spiritual traditions, even amongst those in the Nazis' work and death camps. In the early 1960s, Rabbi Abraham Joshua Heschel dedicated his book, *The Prophets* "To the martyrs of 1940-45," citing Psalm 44:

> *All this has come upon us,*
> *Though we have not forgotten You,*
> *Or been false to Your covenant,*
> *Our heart has not turned back,*
> *Nor have our steps departed from Your way...*
> *For Your sake we are slain . . .*
> *Why do You hide Your face?*
> (Psalm 44:18,19,23,25)

Such fidelity to the traditional, eternal source of Israel's existence defies rational interpretation. The abiding love between Israel and its God is far more a wonder of the world than the lavishness of Solomon's Temple. After World War II, many rabbis were more eloquent in their silence than in proffering words of explanation. Meaning was to be found in the miraculous continuity of Israel's love, the courage of the survivors' enduring faith.

At the same time, whatever they thought of God's power to save, the people of Israel learned that they could not depend on others in this world for their survival. For all that the creation of a nation-state of Israel would leave Jews vulnerable to the temptations of conventional nationalism, after the Holocaust, the physical power of the State of Israel appeared heaven-sent. There is a delicate balance between self-defense and trusting in God. The people of Israel know that they always will be vulnerable to their responsibility as a spiritual people, but they now are more cautious in dealing with the rest of humanity.

The Nazis murdered people whom they deemed unworthy of living because they did not come up to genetic standards established by the Nazis in their own image. Simply put, the Nazis took upon themselves the role of God. In the wake of the genocide of the twentieth century, the survival of humanity is now at stake. Approaching the seventh millennium by Israel's calendar (beginning the third millennium of the common era), the spirituality of Israel remains deep in a process of recovery. Within each of the denominations of Judaism, men, women, and children continue to learn Judaism against a backdrop now of the possibility of Amalek's threatening not only Israel but all of humanity.

Israel grows slowly out of the numbness in which it took refuge in the face of the world's tacit acceptance of the Nazis' plan to exterminate all Jews. The Jewish people now are reawakening to the gifts of their spiritual tradition. As the bloodletting of the twentieth century flows into the twenty-first, Jews have reason to remain cautious in understanding who they are.

Coming in the wake of the Enlightenment's questions about religion *per se*, the experience of the *Shoah* challenged basic assumptions, not only of rabbinical Judaism, but of the original idea of Israel's covenant with God. The vast majority of Jews now lives outside the parameters of the rabbis' understanding of *halakhah*. Large numbers of rabbis themselves pick and choose from the teachings and practices of the ancient rabbis, seeking to meet congregations of Jews in ways to which they can relate. Many Jews do not identify with organized Jewish communities at all.

The State of Israel, affirmed by the United Nations in 1948 when European refugees still were in displaced persons camps under armed guard, is not recognized by most of its neighbors. At the outset of the twenty-first century, traditional hatred of Jews began to reemerge under cover of hatred of the State of Israel. In the summer of 2000, the equation of Zionism with racism was matched by expressions of Nazi-like hatred of the people of Israel at the United Nations' Conference on Racism, held in Durban, South Africa. It was a wake-up call for the people of Israel, putting them back in touch with the anguish that people of color often experience as racism continues to be accepted in many circles.

A thousand years before the Holocaust, Israel knew the difficulty and pain of its spiritual call. An explicator of *Torah* wrote then that, when God identified the divinity of Israel as "I shall be as I shall be," God was saying: "I shall be with them in this sorrow as I shall be with them in other sorrows." After the Holocaust, the people of Israel identify as Jews in many different ways. Some Jews continue to hear Isaiah's ancient call to be a light unto the nations. Some want to live as a "normal" people, with no particular expectations about morality. The vast majority of Jews knows now that basic self respect demands a capacity for self defense.

The existence of an independent, sovereign state with a significant Jewish majority is the source of security for people of Israel around the world. Jews now wake to the ways that historic anti-Semitism is projected onto the State itself. Increasingly, wherever they live, Jews are associated with the nation-state of Israel in the minds of their neighbors. For all the problems that many Jews have about specific tactics or strategies of the Israeli government, there is growing evidence that there is no way for Jews in the Diaspora to disassociate themselves from the State of Israel. All Jews who recognize that their survival and the survival of their children and grandchildren is contingent upon the independence of a Jewish state are essentially people of Israel, whether or not they are citizens of the State of Israel. It is not that Jews have traded in their spiritual tradition for a state. In fact, more Jews today are studying traditional religious texts than ever before in history. Nonetheless, the sad reality is that hatred of Israel persists.

The people of Israel continue to recognize that Israel ultimately is defined by its values and the courage to represent those values in a violent world. Conscience guards this love, as evidenced by the large number of Jews who protest acts of cruelty inflicted by Jews on innocent Palestinians, not to mention the continued concern of Jews for the oppressed and vulnerable around the world. The contemporary struggle of Jews to choose right over wrong was described by Martin Buber in his response in 1938 to Mahatma Gandhi's suggestion that European Jews resist the Nazis nonviolently.

"I cannot help withstanding evil when I see that it is about to destroy the good," Buber wrote to Gandhi. "I am forced to withstand the evil in the world just as the evil within myself. I can only strive not to have to do so by force. I do not want force. But if there is no other way of preventing the evil destroying the good, I trust I shall use force and give myself up into God's hands . . . If I am to confess what is truth to me, I must say: There is nothing better for a man than to deal just-ly–unless it be to love; we should be able even to fight for justice–but to fight lovingly."

The people of Israel fight for the survival of the lifeboat into which they were able to climb after the Nazis were defeated. Israel must depend upon arms because many Arab Moslems insist that the presence of Jews on land once settled by Moslems is a sacrilege. Arab leaders wave the bloodied flag of Palestine, not to end the shedding of blood, but to distract their own peoples from the harsh realities of the tyran-nies to which they are subjected. Israeli creation of settlements on land seized in the Six Day War of 1967 has fed the flames. In the minds of Jews around the world, however, the independence of a sovereign, Jewish state is not negotiable.

It is true that it took Jews a half-century to see the suffering of Arab Palestinians that came with the creation of the State of Israel. Two-thirds of the people of Israel survived the Nazis, but not without suffer-ing the kind of trauma that humanity continues to ignore and thereby abide. Since Israel's invasion of Lebanon in 1982, large numbers of the people of Israel have seen the ways that all of the people living in what once was Canaan continue to be pawns in the struggle of empires. It was the fate of the Palestinians to live on the piece of land to which the Jewish refugees of Europe and the Middle East fled. Arab Palestinians lost their homes, whole villages, their lives. The people of Israel surely know the pain of such loss. When armed with terrible weapons, like everybody else, Jews are open to the temptation of Amalek's murderous logic.

What does it mean to be people of Israel in such a world? What does it mean to wrestle with God when what happened in Europe chal-lenged the very idea of a covenant between Israel and God? Within liv-ing memory of the Holocaust, many in Israel are confused about the idea of Israel's being called at all. Did God really choose Israel? What for? Can the saving power of its God once again drive Israel's experience of itself? What is Israel's role, if any, in responding to the raised thresh-old of pain that human beings abide in the wake of the *Shoah*?

Was not the peoplehood of Israel forged by the harshness of enslavement in Egypt, then by the crushing blow of the Romans who scattered Israel about the face of Earth? As ever, are not the children of Israel at a crossroads in their history, asked not to accept contemporary standards of morality but to raise them?

Struggling With Difference

According to its own stories, the people of Israel play a great role in human history. The Psalmist describes the election of Israel as a new beginning in a cosmic unfolding of the universe:

> When Israel went forth out of Egypt,
> the House of Jacob from a people of an alien language,
> Judah became God's holy nation, Israel God's dominion.
> (Psalm 114:1,2)

What does it mean to be "God's holy nation?" Is not the understanding of one's history as telescoped through the eyes of one's faith tainted by the self-serving perspective of triumphalism?

All through the ages, Israel has distinguished between "God's holy nation" and the other nations. Many of Israel's customs were created to insure the proper growth of "God's people." For example, in biblical times, when the children of Israel first struggled to nurture the ancient religion of Israel, the laws of *kashrut* (dietary laws) were designed to help separate Israel from the rest of the world. As we have seen, the pagan soothsayer, Bilaam, noted this aloneness.

Over the millennia, those who have feared and hated Israel have misunderstood this detachment, misconstrued Israel's claim to being an *am kodesh*, a holy people. Many non-Jews, and not a few Jews, have fallen prey to the notion that the divide between Israel and the other nations was founded on Israel's understanding of itself as better than others.

Jonathan Rosenblum, a brilliant, ultra-orthodox columnist for *The Jerusalem Post*, has identified core issues while writing about events of the day. When the Israeli Supreme Court ruled that the Jewish Agency was not to be allowed to create Jewish-only settlements, Rosenblum asserted that "a degree of separation between Jews and the other nations is a precondition for the fulfillment of our mission. 'A nation that dwells alone,' the Torah calls us." According to Rosenblum, those words "are meant to be prescriptive, not merely descriptive." He recognizes that "all men are created in the image of God, and as such deserving of being treated with dignity." But he cites Rabbi Joseph Soloveitchik as teaching that "Torah emphasizes no less clearly *kedushat* Yisrael, the unique potential for holiness of the Jewish people and the Jews' unique mission as the instruments of God's revelation to the world."

Rosenblum was incensed that Arabs could buy land anywhere in

Israel, while "there are many places where no one would dare sell to a Jew and no Jew would dare to live." He sensed in this Supreme Court ruling a lack of self respect, the old willingness of Jews to be victims. Rosenblum was explicit about his belief that the capacity to love of a Jew is conditioned on a special love for fellow Jews: "Those who can show no special love for their brothers will ultimately show none for others further removed from them, either."

As the people of Israel were harassed and butchered through the centuries, it was not uncommon for them to consider themselves more holy; to distinguish between the circumcised and the uncircumcised as between pure and impure. Such language is striking in medieval chronicles of the Crusades, written by Jews who felt the full force of the teaching of contempt for Jews by the Roman Catholic Church. Living through repeated suicide bombings in the State of Israel, some Jews fall into racism in their depictions of Arabs. Under attack, it is extremely difficult to avoid denigrating the humanity of one's enemy, as Buber suggested in his letter to Gandhi.

But the essence of the tradition of Israel defies such a distinction between people. Created in the image of God, every human being is imbued with the sanctity of holiness. If this is true, what, then, is meant by the idea of *kedushat Yisrael*, the sanctity of Israel? If holiness is holiness, what is Israel's understanding of the holiness of Israel?

The sanctity of Israel is the sanctity of human life. Israel tells the story of humanity in terms of God's relationship with humanity through the witness of the Jewish people. No more than Israel believes that the personhood of Jesus was of a special order, can Israel assert with integrity that its *kedushah* is of a different order from the sanctity of anyone else.

Israel is not taught to be careful about eating because Israel is better than other peoples. Israel is called to eat in certain ways in order to discipline itself to recognize and respect the boundaries of *kashrut*. The boundaries of *kashrut* are not intended to distinguish between Israel and other nations, but rather to remind Israel of its relationship with God.

In the State of Israel, today, this challenge is being played out in terms of the equality of citizenship. Jonathan Rosenblum asks: "What legitimacy can a Jewish state possess if no distinction is permissible between peoples on religious grounds?" The answer is: a Jewish state loses its legitimacy if a distinction about citizenship is permissible on religious grounds. It is reasonable to ask, then, what exactly is the Jewishness of this state?

God willing, sometime in the future, the time will come when the survival and security of the people of Israel will not require the State of Israel to be characterized in any particularly religious way. The Jewishness of the State of Israel is not a principle of Judaism. It is a tactic of the people of Israel, still surrounded by hatred for Jews. The idea of the people of Israel living the religion of Israel in the land of Israel certainly is traditional, but Judaism never was intended to celebrate a state. The people of Israel must walk a fine line between self defense and falling into the triumphalism historically used against them.

In the State of Israel, the Supreme Court's insistence that an Arab family has the right to buy land in an otherwise all Jewish community is a moral choice. It is the same moral choice now facing Jews in the Diaspora who live side-by-side with non-Jews, increasingly within the same families and households. The ghetto of Europe was not a Jewish idea. Independent sovereignty of Jews in the land of Israel was not meant to secure the people of Israel by isolating them. Rather, it was intended to afford Jews the physical and psychic security of not having to worry about being murdered at night, asleep in their beds.

The holiness of "God's holy nation" is dependent upon its people's capacity to see themselves in all their humanity. The hard road that everyone now must travel, if *homo sapiens* is to survive, is an honest encounter with human pride.

Overcoming Pride

A few days before the assassination of Prime Minister Yitzhak Rabin, Rabbi David Hartman prophetically reminded Jews of a teaching of Rabbi Akiba: "Beloved is every human life created in the image of God." Rabbi Hartman cautioned: "The land of Israel becomes holy if, and only if, people live a holy life. We make the land holy by instilling in people the awareness of their being created in the image of God. The land becomes holy when we relate to other people–and peoples–with the understanding that they are carriers of divinity. Israel has returned to the land. Torah remains clear that 'the land belongs to God.'"

For Israel, holiness is created through the struggle to live with respect for oneself and for each other. It is through such striving that Israel mines the spiritual life of the love planted within itself, as it is within every human being. Holiness is not way off somewhere in the sky. "Life is something that visits matter," Rabbi Heschel wrote in 1943, when the future of Israel's life was in question. "It is a transcendent loan, hidden to us . . . We know that something animates and inspirits a living body. But how?"

The answer to the question is to be found in one's attitude towards the world. Israel approaches life as an experience of relationships. The primary relationship is between each one of us and the source of our being (in Israel's case, God). The physical source of our being is our ancestry, the genes of our mother and father and of their parents back on down the line. Physically, we hope for continuity into the future. There is no assurance about how long each of us, the people of Israel, or even humanity as a whole, will survive.

But the spiritual source of our being is not lineal at all. Spirit defies time. Israel is called to remember its spiritual source in order to demonstrate that we humans do have opportunities to survive our own mischief. Having found ways to physically defend itself, Israel needs to reinvigorate its inward life, regenerate its spiritual practice. This is happening in a variety of ways within the various streams of the Jewish people today.

It is not enough that a minority of Jews have returned to study of ancient texts and worship in the synagogue. The reawakening of devotion needs to extend to the vast majority of Jews who still wander about in a cloud of vagueness about who they are as Jews. The ashes of the *Shoah* haven't settled. Many Jews still are essentially dazed. If Judaism is a civilization, as Rabbi Mordechai Kaplan suggests, we are in the midst of the creation of a new stage of the peoplehood of Israel. Perhaps what is happening is the democratization of Israel.

The priestly leadership of ancient Israel was hereditary. Replacing the priesthood, the rabbinate was open to any man with the potential to cultivate what is now called logical/mathematical intelligence. In this respect, rabbinic Judaism is in consonance with the cultural bias widespread in meritocracies today. For the rabbis, all human beings are created in the image of God, but some can get logically/mathematically closer to God than others, particularly through the study of sacred texts. There is a pecking order of intelligence for the rabbis. Simple folk read *t'hillim* (psalms); those with some skills of logic are encouraged to study the *Mishnah;* the elite learn to swim in the logical sophistication of the *Talmud.* The ancient rabbis were careful to leave room for gifts of humility, kindness, and patience, but the temptation to intellectual arrogance was great.

Hasidism began as a protest against this celebration of the intellect. In its contemporary form, however, Hasidism often comes full circle, back to the conceit against which it originally protested. Some Jews now call themselves "neo-hasidic," hearkening back to the spontaneous music and dancing of the original *hasidim*, endeavoring to bring to worship an enthusiasm often absent in contemporary synagogues. The success of their initiative depends upon their ability to transcend the narcissism of contemporary culture. The danger is that they worship Jewish peoplehood (themselves) rather than God.

As Ernest Kurtz and Katherine Ketcham teach in *The Spirituality of Imperfection: Storytelling and the Journey to Wholeness*, spirituality grows in the discovery of real listening. "To obey means simply to 'listen thoroughly.'" Jews most likely to be part of a revived spirituality will be those who really listen, to themselves, to other Jews, to human beings, to the cry of the universe. Abraham and Sarah listened. Moses and the children of Israel listened. The prophets listened. The sages of Israel listened, even if they eventually voted. The traditional spirituality of Israel is founded on hearing the command *(mitzvah): "Shema Yisrael, Hear O Israel, the Lord our God is One."*

Where are the good listeners to be found? In every neighborhood of Israel, amongst all the streams of Judaism, as well as in the homes of Jews off on their own, often in the quiet desperation of knowing themselves to be children of Israel, yet unable to find a way to identify with a larger Jewish world. Most Jews today are waiting for the cultural landscape to change. The question of the authority of the rabbis is a red herring. Millions of Jews recognize that they live in the thundering wake of the Holocaust and the creation of the third Jewish commonwealth, and that the rabbis are struggling to retain what little leadership they retain. Nonetheless, as regard for the literature of the rabbis is restored in ways that are unrelated to the legal claims of rabbis to be stewards of the personal and communal behavior of Israel, the treasures of both Judaism and the biblical religion of Israel are appealing to creative souls intent on nurturing the traditional sense of responsibility and duty upon which spiritual freedom depends.

Revivals of learning take time, going hand in hand with the growth of personal and communal practice. The character of the motivation for this cultural development will determine the direction it takes. The purpose of the reclamation of knowledge of traditional Jewish study and practice cannot afford to be tainted with common national pretensions. The traditional motivation for Jewish learning is acknowledgment of the spiritual source of all knowledge. Israel must wean itself of its intellectual self-satisfaction. Too much of the contemporary revival of learning and practice is fed by a sense of self-importance that one would expect to find amongst a people still embattled. That this self-satisfaction is understandable, however, does not mitigate its danger.

After the Maccabean rebellion and the reclaiming of sovereignty by the Hasmoneans in the second century b.c.e., the Second Commonwealth of Israel expanded aggressively. The increase in size was not solid growth, for it was conditioned by an imperial pride that robbed Israel of memory of the righteousness of the original revolt of the Maccabees. Likewise, Israel's physical strength today will be for nought if the people of Israel forget the source of their survival and rebirth. Power and powerlessness both corrupt. The people of Israel must help identify a third way. Israel, being Israel, cannot expect to live without reclaiming its role as a beacon for humanity.

Given the physical strength of the State of Israel, it is difficult for many non-Jews to understand the persistently high level of Jewish insecurity. Recovery from attempted genocide takes generations. As a defense against the pain of such healing, national pride only gets in the way of a people's moving on. There are reasons for Jews to wonder about the commitment of the world to their well being. Israel's traditional teachings about God's kindness often ring hollow in the face of indisputable, living memory. The ancient rabbis themselves had their doubts about God. In the end, however, the sages of Israel knew that they could not avoid Israel's spiritual challenge. They called the pain for which they could not account "sufferings of love," the ache endured just in being human.

Every healthy culture has its own understanding of "sufferings of love." The experience of inexplicable pain is an eternal challenge to the mind of humanity. Responding to this challenge is an opportunity for human beings to reject facile explanations and accept instead that *homo sapiens* cannot understand all of its experience. This acknowledgment is critical to the struggle to overcome pride.

It is folly to ignore all the unnecessary pain that we human beings inflict on each other. It is no sign of weakness, however, to accept the sufferings of love, come when they may. Human beings must learn to distinguish between the unnecessary infliction of pain and the sufferings of love that, even as they hurt, make tender the human heart, enlarging its capacity for kindness and love.

Chosen for What?

The crisis for Israel today is reflected in the bitterness of the debate amongst the people of Israel. Charges of heresy and treason, racism and tyranny are not uncommon. Jews of differing perspectives accuse each other of internalized anti-Semitism. No one group of Jews, wherever it is on religious and cultural spectrums, has a clear partial picture, let alone the whole picture, of the ideas and practices of Israel following the catastrophe of the twentieth century. Israel's struggle reflects the challenge for human beings as a whole. The links between the survival of Israel and the survival of humanity are becoming more explicit, calling Israel to remember its responsibility on Earth. Israel is well positioned by its history and the nature of its peoplehood to address the evils of greed and racism that threaten the equilibrium of life on this planet.

Israel's ultimate value is, not the survival of Jews, but their willingness to continue to live as servants of God. Much of the attention of the leadership of Israel today, on the part of rabbis and the philanthropists who set the agenda of secular organizations, is focused on the survival of Israel. At times, it would appear that Israel's leaders have forgotten the counsel of Rabbi Yohanan Ha-Sandlar in *Pirkei Avot*: "Every assembly whose purpose is to serve God will in the end be established; but every assembly whose purpose is not for God's sake, will not in the end be established." *(Pirkei Avot 4:14)*

The ultimate value of the *State* of Israel as a nation-state is its own survival, the physical protection of its people. The *spiritual people* of Israel, however, exist not to perpetuate their own existence, but to serve God. Israel is a people called into existence by the God of Israel. Anthropologically speaking, the story makes sense. Peoples tend to see themselves as creations of their own gods. Remove God from the picture of Israel and its character as a spiritual nation melts away.

The danger that the State of Israel will be but one more nation-state, defending its own people at all costs, is a threat to both Israel and all humanity. The State of Israel does exist to defend itself. The people of Israel are here for a greater purpose.

Unfortunately, some Jews today, are unable to see beyond their own fear and pain. They succumb to the pride of their triumphalism. Ironically, they reflect the mirror image of Jews who are embarrassed by the notion that Israel is called by God to a spiritual mission. Both the triumphalists and those who try to ignore the record of Israel's historic responsibility for moral leadership would settle for survival for the sake of survival.

For those whose identity as Jews is shaped by the spiritual ideas of Israel, the notion of Israel as chosen to serve God is integral to Jewish identity. Even those religious Jews who have adapted the liturgy to exclude language about Israel being "chosen from among the nations," continue to speak of Israel being "chosen for the service of God." In Rabbi Heschel's eloquent words: "Israel exists not in order to be, but in order to cherish the vision of God. Our faith may be strained but our destiny is anchored to the ultimate. Who can establish the outcome of our history? Out of the wonder we came and into the wonder we shall return."

More often than not, the experience of serving God is to be found in the small moments of eternity we encounter as we seek to live freely. Insisting on the creation of a just peace, in our own lives and throughout the world, we often find ourselves struggling. From the beginning, with whatever name they identified, the people of Israel have wrestled with God. As we have seen, at first they were *b'nai Yaakov*, the children of Jacob, *bayt Yisrael*, the house of Israel. Jacob was called Israel for wrestling with what haunted him. In Egypt, the children of Israel were called Hebrews, "ones who crossed over." Rabbinical Judaism took the idea of Israel and turned it into Judaism. In the process, what it meant to be an individual wrestler with God changed in some significant ways. One was no longer an Israelite but a Jew. After the return from Babylonia, Jewish peoplehood was defined less existentially and more ethnically. Guided by the rabbis' genius and wisdom, the people of Israel continued to grow through two millennia, surviving the fall of two Temples and the loss of the security of their own state in the land of Israel. As they wandered Earth, they remembered their spiritual mission.

Then came the *Shoah*, and the recreation of a State of Israel in the land of Israel. The nature of the security of Israel for Jews who live in the State of Israel is different from the nature of security for Jews in the Diaspora. Though the citizens of the state clearly are not physically secure, there is a world of difference between living as a Jew in Tel Aviv today and living as a Jew in Warsaw before, during, or after World War II. The reasons are obvious. Jews in the State of Israel are better armed, and there are well tested forms of civil and military leadership built into a state.

Even so, many citizens of the State of Israel continue to struggle with the religion of Judaism and its traditional leaders, the rabbis. In the State of Israel, there is special status accorded Orthodox rabbis whose fundamentalist interpretation of the spiritual tradition of Israel is foreign, not only to most Israelis but also to many Jews who consider themselves to be observant of religious Judaism. To what extent will the people of Israel continue to be ruled by this fundamentalism? Throughout the world, most Jews live outside the boundaries of fundamentalist interpretation of Jewish law and custom.

Millions of Jews now seek an authentic experience of Israel. As hard as they may try to escape the uniqueness of their calling, they cannot uproot their personal sense of experiencing their humanity as people of Israel. Knowing themselves as Jews, they wonder for what they were chosen. Just as the religion of ancient Israel became Judaism when the Second Temple was destroyed, Judaism now needs to open to a transformation that will provide the people of Israel with the spiritual sustenance they seek. The basic structure of rabbinical Judaism has weakened. So much of the law and custom of the traditional *halakhah* is irrelevant to most Jews. Efforts to revive the old *halakhah* come into conflict repeatedly with new moral standards, particularly concerning authority and gender.

The spiritual tradition of Israel now must become democratic, continuing to honor Israel's leaders for their wisdom, but sharing political power equally amongst all Jews. It is past time for the insights of Jewish feminism to shape the mainstream. Feminism's critique of patriarchy extends beyond issues of gender equity to the understanding of power in relationships.

All of Israel must engage in debate about the interface between the democratic spirit and monotheism. Here is an opportunity for Israel to model for humanity an honest encounter with the limits of *homo sapiens* to control our own destiny. What does it mean to proclaim God's sovereignty? Why do so many people cringe at the traditional idea of being a servant, indeed, a slave of God *(eved ha'shem)*? Imagine the creativity of a debate in which Jews from all streams of Israel were to listen carefully to each other.

It is time to think of generating a new "way" for Israel, as firmly grounded in the ancient rabbis' Judaism as their Judaism was grounded in the ancient religious tradition of Israel. The people of Israel today must have the courage and imagination of their ancient sages. The condition of humanity begs for Israel to come into a new way of living that bears witness to its ancient call to serve.

Halakhah and Aggadah

Chaim Nachman Bialik (1873-1934) was Israel's poet laureate in the years when Zionism was a movement, the revival of sovereignty still a dream. He was a student of *Hebrew Scriptures* and the sacred texts of the rabbis, but he chose to live his life outside the parameters of the rabbi's interpretation of *halakhah*. It is unlikely that any child of Israel was more thoroughly a Jew.

Bialik wrote a seminal essay, *Halakhah* and *Aggadah*, in which he described brilliantly the two sides of the coin of the culture of Israel: *halakah*, the customs and laws, and *aggadah*, the stories, the lore. "*Halakhah* wears a frown," he wrote, "*aggadah* a smile. The one is pedantic, severe, unbending–all justice; the other is accommodating, lenient, pliable–all mercy."

Bialik understood that "*[h]alakhah* is the crystallization, the ultimate and inevitable quintessence, of *aggadah; aggadah* is the substance of *halakhah. Aggadah* is the plaintive voice of the heart's yearning as it wings its way to its haven; *halakhah* is the resting-place, where for a moment the yearning is satisfied and stilled. As a dream seeks its fulfillment in interpretation, as will in action, as thought in speech, as flower in fruit–so *aggadah* in *halakhah*. But in the pith of the fruit there lies hidden the seed from which a new flower will grow. The *halakhah* which is sublimated into a symbol–and such *halakhah* exists, as we shall find–becomes the mother of a new *aggadah*, which may or may not be like it. A living and healthy *halakhah* is an *aggadah* that has been or that will be."

We cannot live without air to breathe and solid ground upon which to stand. In the concrete acts of living, our need for air and solid ground always are directly related. "*Aggadah* gives us air to breathe, *halakhah* gives us solid ground to stand on." Healthy culture requires customs and law as well as legends and lore. The problem, today, is that the culture of Israel is divided against itself. One part of Israel is desperate for air to breathe; another part looks for solid ground upon which to stand. Traditionalists are tempted to worship the law, rather than God. Jews who are more accepting of contemporary culture are afraid to venture forth beyond quaint stories about justice and compassion. Far too few in Israel today accept fully the necessity of the claims of both *halakhah* and *aggadah*. Indeed, there is little opportunity for dialogue between those who are gasping for air and those who cannot stay on their feet.

In his essay, Bialik concluded that what was needed was a deepened sense of responsibility, of personal duty. Orthodoxy tends to impose upon all of Israel the entire system of behavior and belief of the ancient rabbis. Those who reject this rabbinical claim tend to leave to each person all the choices and ways to practice being a Jew. There are people at all points on the spectrum who have their own deep understanding of personal duty, whether in traditional or non-traditional terms.

It may be that the fissures are too deep. At times in the past, the people of Israel have divided, some going forward on roads leading to new ways of identifying and innovative forms of practice; others condemned to walk towards one of history's dead-ends. Defenders of the Temple cult are largely gone, though there are a few in Jerusalem today who scheme to clear the Temple Mount of its two mosques. The ancient rabbis gave the priests and Levites a few minor responsibilities in rabbinical Judaism. For example, in the synagogue service, they are first to be called to the *Torah* when it is publicly read. At the same time, the rabbis made clear their presumption that the identity of the priesthood as a whole was subject to doubt.

There is a need for greater courage in all camps, a willingness to imagine how the people of Israel can break through to a shared understanding of *mitzvah* (commandment) that they can embrace with the passion upon which Bialik's healthy sense of duty depends. The non-traditional insist on their personal freedom, even as they wonder about their own authenticity as Jews. The Orthodox cling to *halakhah*, even as they project their own doubt about their certainty into the eyes of those they call heretics. The people of Israel have enough enemies already; they cannot afford to continue to play such games.

Mitzvah *in* Torah

The sages of Israel defined a commandment as one of the 613 particular *mitzvot* (commandments) which they identified as the substance of *halakhah*. But *mitzvah* had a different meaning in biblical times. As we have seen, Moses spoke of *mitzvah* when he bid farewell to the people as they were about to enter the promised land. *(Deuteronomy 29-30)* His words from *Torah* are read in synagogue on the Shabbat preceding Rosh Hashanah and Yom Kippur, days of awe when many in Israel still gather to search their souls. There is tremendous drama about these verses which poured out of Israel's greatest prophet who spoke from his depths as he approached his own death.

After suggesting that God would open the hearts of all those assembled, as well as the hearts of their children, Moses sought to reassure the people that being faithful to the covenant would not be a difficult task. He said: "For this *mitzvah* that I have commanded you today, it is not hidden from you, nor is it far off. It is not in the heavens, that you would say, 'Who will go up for us to the heavens and get it for us, that we may hear it and observe it?' And it is not across the sea, that you would say: 'Who will go across the sea for us, and get it for us, that we may hear it and observe it?' For the word is very near to you, in your mouth and in your heart, that you may do it. See, I set before you, today, life and good, and death and evil; in that I command you today to love the Eternal One, your God, to walk in God's ways, and to keep God's commandments (*mitzvotav*) and statutes (*v'hukotav*) and legal judgments (*u'mishpatav*), that you may live and multiply, and the Eternal One your God, may bless you in the land that you are entering to possess."

While translation of the words *hukah* and *mishpat* is open to debate, there is no ambiguity about *mitzvah*. It clearly has the sense of commandment. It is true that, through Yiddish, the word came to have a folk meaning of "good deed," perhaps as ethnic identity filled in for weakening religious ties. But in *Hebrew Scriptures*, as we have seen here in *Deuteronomy, mitzvah* speaks of divine commandment.

In the verses cited here from *Deuteronomy*, "this *mitzvah*" is described as a word of command to be found not far away, but "in your mouth, in your heart, to do it." This was biblical Israel's understanding of *mitzvah*, very different from the rabbis' notion of the 613 particular *mitzvot* which comprised their teaching of *halakhah*. Before the rabbis, commandment in *Torah* had a sense of a personal experience of conscience. Obviously, the individual Israelite in biblical times was not free, in a twenty-first century sense, of the norms, customs, and laws of family and society. The point is that Israel's understanding of *mitzvah* has changed in the past and can continue to evolve.

In *Halakhah* and *Aggadah*, Bialik complained about a Judaism "of mere phrases and catchwords, and a kind of do-as-you-please Judaism." He derided the way that the cultural expressions of the people of Israel of his time were "hang[ing] by the gossamer thread of some kind of love–love of the land, love of the language, love of the literature." He asked: "Love? Where is duty? Whence can it come? What does it mean to live?" Bialik saw Israel's desperate need for "molds in which we can mint our unformed will into solid coin that will endure. We long for something concrete."

Lest he be misunderstood as yearning for the reimposition of traditional rabbinical practice, Bialik said explicitly: "Are we then to return to such legal codes as the *Shulhan Arukh* [the sixteenth century compilation of *halakhah*]? To interpret my words in this way, is to misunderstand them completely." Bialik was calling for Jews to have a greater sense of duty that would be expressed in action. But he knew full well (the way he lived his life as a Jew bore witness to this understanding) that what was needed was not the reimposition of a form of *halakhah* to which the vast majority of the people of Israel no longer could relate. The sense of duty for which Bialik cried would come with the regeneration of a new *halakhah* out of a revived *aggadah*. "A living and healthy *halakhah*," he wrote, "is an *aggadah* that has been or that will be."

Bialik recognized the centrality to Israel of *mitzvah*, the sense of personal duty that lives in one's mouth and heart, the kind of obligation described more often in our time as conscience than obedience to God, though the obedience to God that Moses taught at the end of *Torah* can also be interpreted as the free working of personal conscience. The reason for our contemporary struggle with such language of duty is that, for thousands of years, religious authority saw fit to limit or forbid the free working of personal conscience. The advocates of the Enlightenment of the eighteenth and nineteenth centuries raised their voices, risked their lives, by walking into the face of the variety of religious tyrannies which defined European culture and were transplanted to the American colonies. At that point in time, more light was to be found in reason's critique of the superstition of religion (ecclesiastical tyranny being one of its more dangerous manifestations) than in expressions of the spirit that betrayed the freedom inherent in the religious idea.

Is it not time for all of us who cherish freedom to unite, whether our understanding of the sacred is traditionally religious or fruit of the struggles of reason? We already stand on the common ground of our insistence on the primacy of conscience. We need to understand better the ways in which we allow our different languages of discourse to divide us.

Nowhere is this truer than amongst the people of Israel. It is important that the people of Israel recognize the ways that *halakhah* and *aggadah* are two sides of the same coin; important, as well, that they stop flinching in the face of the sexism, authoritarianism and ethnocentrism of the old *halakhah*. Once a new idea that transformed Israel so that the people of Israel would survive, the traditional *halakhah* is now more concrete vault than living and breathing tradition.

RECLAIMING THE PROMISE

After Rabbinical Judaism

Like *Hebrew Scriptures*, rabbinical Judaism is an interpretation of the idea of Israel that the people of Israel always will cherish. To what extent the ancient rabbis' *midrash* (interpretation) will continue to bear witness to who Israel is will be determined by how the rabbinical tradition is now mined. The destruction of the Second Temple in 70 c.e. was a clear turning point, but the transition at that time from the religion of ancient Israel to Judaism was a process, as cultural movement tends to be. Israel today is in the midst of such a long-term change.

The *Shoah* and the recreation of independent Jewish sovereignty would appear to make for a great divide. What remains to be seen is whether or not the regeneration of Israel in our time will be accompanied by the appearance of a new leadership group, like the rabbis, who built Judaism in the shell of the old Israel of the Levites. In a democratic age, the people of Israel can be expected to insist on the full rights of personal conscience, even as they may continue to look to the wisdom of a heterogeneous group of rabbis.

At this point, the rabbinate is bitterly divided. As the priest Ezra seemed to see over the horizon the coming of a great change, many rabbis now sense the bankruptcy of the idea of their right to determine the morality of the personal behavior of Jews. It is too early to know even the outlines of what is to come, but it is past time for the people of Israel to be imaginative and bold in envisioning the continued growth of Judaism. Even this name, Judaism, which replaced the name Israel when the rabbis came on the scene, may be outliving its time. Perhaps, once again, wherever they live, Jews will be known as the people who walk the way of Israel, allowing the traditions of its calendar to shape their lives, day by day, year after year.

Many Jews today are struggling to relate to the uniqueness of their identity. The idea that one people is holy and another is not is anathema, not only to Enlightenment values, but to the spiritual tradition of Israel itself. Certainly it can be found in Israel's history, from ancient days through our own time, but the weakness of such thinking is widely acknowledged today.

Israel now is challenged to continue to grow. After the genocide of the twentieth century and the recreation of independent Jewish sovereignty, the people of Israel are in a unique position to advance human understanding of nationality so that each nation knows itself as equally unique and uniquely equal. It is not by claiming that Israel is better that the people of Israel model their uniqueness. There is nothing unique about the claim of superiority; it's just the same old game that has given both religion and nationalism such bad names. The uniqueness of each child of Israel (as the uniqueness of every human being) is forged by his or her seeking out, with full heart, soul and might, the depths of his or her own personal experience, embracing the unconditional love at the heart of who he or she is. Is it not the task of the people of the spiritual nation of Israel to bear witness to all that stands in the way of humanity's survival?

Jewish history is a record of generation after generation of the people of Israel devoting their lives, sacrificing their lives, precisely for the purpose of serving their God of justice and compassion. It would be a betrayal of all the courage and loss for Israel now to become just another player in the old national game. It also would increase the odds that the universe will unfold without *homo sapiens.*

It will be risky for Israel fully to come out of the closet as a spiritual nation. Risk is not new for Israel. What is new, after two thousand years, is the cultural possibility afforded by the existence of a political state within which the prevailing religious tradition is Judaism. The State of Israel not only protects the physical security of the people of Israel; its political power offers the people of Israel an opportunity to dive into its spiritual responsibility with the freedom that has defined the spiritual tradition of Israel from the beginning.

The existence of the State of Israel raises the stakes for people of Israel living in the Diaspora. The mixed ethnic and racial demography of the Jews who are citizens of the State of Israel reminds all Jews of the mixed seed of their people. A thousand years ago, in response to a letter from a convert to Judaism, Maimonides insisted that the truth about the seed of Israel is spiritual, not physical. The point was driven home before the world's eyes when the State of Israel airlifted the Jews of Ethiopia to their promised land.

In seventeenth-century New England, Roger Williams spoke of the people of the new world as the "mixed seed of Israel." Israel's seed is inherently mixed because, ultimately, Israel is not about humans being of a particular ethnicity or even living in one land. Israel is a spiritual people who bear witness to their nationality by serving God. Of course, Jews of color continue to struggle to integrate into the culture of Israel.

Racism is universal; Jews are not exempt. But the nature of Israel's seed, the fact that, in its essence, it is founded in acceptance of the yoke of serving God rather than in common ancestry, cries out now to the people of Israel with an answer to their question, "Chosen for what?" God willing, Jews all over the world will rise to the challenge of responding to this question, demonstrating for all of humanity the capacity to transcend fully the bigotries surrounding physical differences.

Memories of the common ancestry of Abraham's children, of Ishmael and Isaac, call out for such reconciliation. Some day, if *homo sapiens* does survive–indeed, if humans are to survive—Israel will have to open itself to the full universality of its own vision. The point of the murderous triumphalism of September 11th, 2001, is that the opening must begin now. There are significant ways for each of the historic spiritual traditions of the world to move away from placing primary value on their own survival, returning instead to answer the call that first brought them into being. It is the pride of humanity that threatens our survival and the survival of Earth. It is Israel's mission (and the mission of all others as well) to speak to that pride.

Rainfall and Torah

A couple of thousand years ago, a Greek philosopher asked Rabbi Joshua ben Chananiah:

"At what time are all people equal, and when do the nations come to worship together?"

Rabbi Joshua replied:

"On the day when all rejoice."

"When is that?" asked the philosopher.

"When the heavens have been shut up, and all are in distress, and the rain comes down, and all rejoice and praise God."

Then Rabbi Tanhum ben Chiyya spoke up. Well ahead of his own time, yet, God willing, not ours, he asserted:

"The falling of the rain is greater than the giving of *Torah*, for the giving of *Torah* was a joy only to Israel, while the falling of the rain is a rejoicing for all the world's peoples, as well as the cattle and the wild beasts and the birds." Imagine such a statement being made two thousand years ago. It is testament to the deep roots of Judaism's teaching of the universality of the fulfillment of its ancient promises.

The initial statement of Rabbi Joshua also speaks to the generosity of the vision of the ancient rabbis. All the nations will worship God when the heavens open up and all rejoice and praise God. It is more than likely that Rabbi Joshua was thinking of everyone praising the God of Israel, which is what makes Rabbi Tanhum's words so radical, for they speak of a vision in which even *Torah*, Israel's understanding of God's Teaching, is secondary to the falling of the rain.

Alas, today it is no longer so simple. Remember what happened after the nuclear accident at Chernobyl? All around the world, people waited with dread for the Chernobyl cloud to make its way through the atmosphere. Nobody wanted rain. Neither Rabbi Joshua nor Rabbi Tanhum could conceive of a time when the very rain would be such a mortal threat.

Maybe we can play with their words. Perhaps they got it backwards, that all rejoice when the rains come down and praise God. Perhaps it will take our praise of God, in every language by which human beings reflect on the spiritual source of all, to lead us to clean up the rain. We can adjust Rabbi Tanhum's statement, then, retaining its intent, while turning it around. The giving of *Torah* is greater than the falling of rain, both because we now have to worry about what we have done to the rain, and because the giving of *Torah* to Israel is a rejoicing for all the world–when human beings understand that the giving of *Torah* to Israel is one of many ways of describing the goal of humans to live in freedom.

The Story Points to Integrity

Israel is an idea of humanity that is projected onto a people. The idea is a promise of a way of living that can be described as *integrity*, the wholeness of what the human mind is designed to break into pieces, like us and them, subject and object. A human tale, the story of Israel necessarily speaks of humanity in terms of parts, Israel and the other nations. The challenge is to interpret this story in ways that point towards the union of being that is inherent in humanity.

After the twentieth century, human beings sense a great need for unity. In our haste, though, we often neglect to distinguish between a physical unity imposed from without and the spiritual union that grows from within: the difference between the subdued tension of the absence of war and the meditative quiet of inner peace. Israel was called into being in order to lift up a vision for humanity, and this vision can be realized only through a spiritual process that comes from within.

Hatred of Israel is sparked by the sensitivity of such introspection, the difficulty of the struggle to distinguish between the modesty of self-respect and the humiliation of self-hate.

Integrity is a state of self-acceptance that is founded on the recognition of the indeterminacy of love. God asked Abraham and Sarah to trust in a divine caring for which there never is absolute proof. At Mount Sinai, God did not choose Israel once and for all time. As long as Israel sees itself as a people, every moment of every day and night, Jews are asked to accept that there is nothing certain about God's offer other than its indeterminacy. God asks Israel to embrace the goodness of life, the potential for love in human existence.

Never given conclusive proof of such a potential, Israel is expected to model, through its own living, the possibility for us humans to trust in this loving ground of our experience. This is the divine service for which Israel was chosen. For two thousand years, without a land or state of its own, Israel served with distinction, not as a victim of human tyranny, but as a model of spiritual peoplehood. With a land and a state now, the mission remains the same.

How can human beings grow into a respect for themselves that comes from within and not at the expense of other people? How can humanity learn to bet on a flowering of its potential for love? It is no accident that, after the twentieth century, Jews are asked to take this chance. It is Israel's calling. What is different now is that Israel no longer accepts the role of being the canary in the mine. The fate of Israel and the destiny of all humanity are now more closely tied. God willing, it will increasingly be seen that the extended family of Israel is humanity.

Extended Family of Israel

When the people of Israel came home to the land of Israel, there was much rejoicing. The connection between the land and the people goes back to Abraham and Sarah, almost four thousand years. Yet, of even greater significance is the equally ancient spiritual connection between the people of Israel and the God of Israel. Imagine the rejoicing when the standards of justice and compassion of the God of Israel are celebrated as the essence of the folkways and customs of the people of the world.

Actually, Jews have rejoiced over the decency of such living all through their journey. The Jewish calendar is a cycle of days of such rejoicing, day to day in expressions of gratitude to God, week to week in the serenity of *Shabbat*, around the year in festive rituals. Grounded in home and synagogue, the continuity of this calendar has defied murderous assault. It is tested today by a transformation of our understanding of family.

It was the genius of Ezra and the ancient rabbis to shape the tradition in ways that deepened the ties of Israel's spiritual understanding to the ethnic loyalties of Jews wherever they lived. All of Israel shared one calendar; each community was free to create and transmit to successive generations its own *midrash* on this calendar. One does not need to visit museums to encounter the beauty of the texture and depth of these ethnic cultures, which continue to find expression in the real lives of Jews today.

Yet, *homo sapiens* now is in the midst of a great transformation. Technical and organizational revolutions have afforded human beings unprecedented mobility and communication. Within a few generations, many traditional ethnic cultures *will* find more expression in museums than in living communities.

History records humanity's struggle to maintain a creative balance between endogamy and ethnic intermarriage. Given the spiritual dimensions of *homo sapiens,* however, there is a limit to the truth of ethnic understandings. Murderous expressions of racism in the twentieth century signaled the risk in ethnic thinking to the life of humanity as a whole. After the twentieth century, all nations will have to confront the configuration of their self-understanding.

The struggle can be seen today within native American culture. The gambling deals which tribal elders have made with state governments depend upon an understanding of nationality based upon ethnicity. It will not take many generations before fewer and fewer native people qualify for a share of the gambling receipts. When the number gets small enough, one can expect that state and federal governments will assert their authority, and the last bit of native American sovereignty effectively will disappear.

As a consequence, younger leaders have rejected a blood-based definition of nationality. They want to return to more existential ways of defining their peoplehood. Traditionally, after living with a tribe for a long time, one became a member of the tribe. No doubt, there were rites of initiation, but the divide between those who were born of the nation and those who were welcomed was much less important than existential participation in the ways of the tribe. Boundaries were drawn from the inside out, rather than the outside in.

Leaders of nations and religions are suspicious of growth that is inside out, for it is more difficult for them to control. As a rule, people in control want to stay in control. And the sad truth is that the fate of humanity and Earth never was more out of *homo sapiens'* control. Old understandings of human organization from the top down and the outside in are bankrupt. There are many poignant examples of the danger of this situation. Even as human beings have learned to produce enough food and shelter for all, large numbers of people continue to starve and suffer malnutrition. Millions of refugees of war wander about Earth. In the wealthiest societies, homelessness is accepted as a given.

Today's struggle of the people of Israel to define their nation's identity is another example of human beings' straining to survive in our time. In the beginning, the standard of Israelite identity was both patrilineal and existential. As already noted, Abraham circumcised every male in the camp, whether or not they were blood relations. Isaac was an Israelite both because he was Abraham's child and because he lived his life in accord with the spiritual tradition of his people.

The existential factor of living the life always has allowed non-blood relations to become members of the people of Israel, even as the rabbis switched the standard from patrilineal to matrilineal. The situation changed late in the twentieth century when the numbers of Jews who were marrying non-Jews increased substantially. This was not the first time that Judaism needed to absorb large numbers of converts. In the early days of rabbinical Judaism, in Greco-Roman times, the numbers of Israel were greatly augmented by people choosing to be Jews. But the social and political situation then was very different from that of the late twentieth century, when Jews were accorded all the rights of democratic citizenship, and the loyalty of the people of Israel to their own traditional calendar was wavering.

When the rabbis of Reform Judaism decided, in 1983, to validate either matrilineal or patrilineal identity, as long as the person agreed to be educated and live as a Jew, the standard of identity of the people of Israel was complicated. Both Conservative and Orthodox rabbis made it clear that they did not accept the patrilineal standard. As a consequence, in some communities of Jews, there are now genealogical records being preserved, and people raised as Jews by Reform standards are not considered Jews by many Conservative and Orthodox authorities. With large numbers of Jews today not affiliated with any organized Jewish community, many who consider themselves people of Israel would not be accepted as Jews in many synagogues. The situation only will get more difficult and hurtful.

Is it not time for Israel to sacrifice ethnicity as a determinant of its identity? Through much of its history, ethnicity has well served the idea of Israel. But there is a time and a place for everything. It may be that, in choosing intermarriage over endogamy, the majority of Jews in the Diaspora are leading Israel towards its future, rather than turning their backs on Israel, as their critics bitterly complain.

Once a creative source of personal identity, ethnicity would appear to have exhausted itself as an instrument of human culture. As human beings intermarry, the vitality of ethnic loyalties is tested. What once seemed respectful begins to touch on hubris and even racism. With humanity now at the precipice of its own existence, the people of Israel are called to jettison the scaffolding of ethnicity that has served as a measure of their identity. Israel now is asked to depend entirely on its way of life as a determinant of who it is as a people.

Such a radical change will not be easy. It will require the courage of Abraham and the laughter of Sarah, the faith of Moses, the wisdom and patience of the ancient rabbis. However, it is far from a crap shoot. Does not the essence of God's teaching of *Torah* celebrate difference as a precondition for the possibility of the growth of integrity? Taken a little too far, is not ethnic loyalty ultimately idolatrous?

The fact that, after almost four thousand years, there is no agreement about "who is a Jew," may reflect not social incompetence, but the truth that one can no more understand the identity of Israel than one can understand the God of Israel. The people of Israel have their own calendar; indeed, as Rabbi Kaplan taught, their own civilization. In the end, however, if a Jew is true to the God of Israel, a Jew must recognize that, ultimately, he or she is a human being; the people of Israel, humanity.

Israel is not a brand. Israel is a calling of humanity that has grown and changed significantly over four thousand years. From the beginning, the defining experience of Israel was the desire to hear God's command to humanity to act in such ways that it may live justly in peace. Israel is *homo sapiens* called to moral decision-making. Of course, there are other peoples who try to live righteously. The people of Israel are not alone in having time-tested ways of living with a consciousness of moral obligation. Many peoples have their own calendars and civilizations. May all human beings now lift up the spiritual dimensions of their own self-understandings.

Christians today, who have an understanding of Jesus that fits well within the prophetic tradition of Israel, consider themselves members of the people of Israel. Jews need to greet them as they walk together on related paths. In the process, it would be healthy for all friends of the Jewish people to reflect on the significance of the continued struggle of the people of Israel to survive in the Middle East where they have gathered in great numbers after the Holocaust.

In the course of their histories, both the religion of ancient Israel and rabbinical Judaism always have looked to family as the primary teacher. It is safe to say that Israel is no different from any nation in this regard. Families of Jews today are as stressed as other families. Popular culture competes with parents and teachers to shape the values of children. The need to have two breadwinners in a household leaves children vulnerable to influences of which the most vigilant parents are not aware.

Given the close relationship between ethnicity and family, it would seem to be an inopportune time to sever the links between ethnicity and Judaism. But the hard reality is that these connections already are eroding. For all of the desire and efforts to hold onto knowledge of Yiddish and Ladino, these folk languages no longer are the bases of living cultures. Large numbers of converts to Judaism are redefining the ethnicity of Israel in the Diaspora.

Along with the growth of this ethnic melting pot, families of Jews are being transformed by the gender revolution which is sweeping through the developed world. In many ways, men retain much of their traditional control, but the balance of the family certainly is shifting. Changes in the understanding of gender are more exponential than most of us realize. The rights of women to participate equally in the liturgy of the synagogue and in the Jewish world at large are now recognized even within parts of Orthodoxy, though Judaism knows the same intensity of reaction to ideas about equality of gender as can be found in other religious traditions. It is a fierce battle on a number of fronts, including a struggle over how to imagine God and conceive of religious authority.

The Hebrew language has the power to hold together the *mishpahah* (family) of Israel. Hebrew is the language through which Israel hears God's command. The people of Israel need to reclaim an appreciation of the beauty of the poetry of Hebrew prayer. The revival of Hebrew as the spoken language of the people of Israel can be matched by a recognition, on the part of Jews and the world at large, of the potential of Hebrew to ground a cultural renaissance, much as Greek and Latin have in the past. Far more than remnants of the old ethnic cultures, a few words of Yiddish or an Eastern European recipe, knowledge of Hebrew can be instrumental as the language of Israel's spiritual revival as well as its physical rebirth in the land of Israel.

The power of Hebrew, recognized by Christians during their Renaissance, was noted as well by the founders of American culture who included the study of Hebrew in the curriculum of the first universities in the United States. For Jews themselves, Hebrew offers direct access to more than three millennia of their people's experience. Hebrew is the foundation of Jewish civilization. "Once Hebrew becomes a foreign or ancient tongue to the Jew," Rabbi Mordechai Kaplan wrote, "he ceases to experience any intimacy with Jewish life." The revival of Hebrew as a living language was built into the creation of the modern State of Israel. For Jews, however, the power of Hebrew transcends the State of Israel, providing the people of Israel with their right of entry to the wonders of the universe.

Israel and Culture

Inasmuch as one can stand naked before God, true to the idea of Israel, one does not know of ethnic, racial, or even religious ideas. Ethnicity, race, and religion are humanly devised concepts of culture. They can be strong, describing very personal ways of identifying as a human being. In the presence of the divine, however, ethnicity, race, and religion are half-truths that make it difficult for us to experience the indivisibility of life.

Human identity is at once both particular and universal. The religion of Israel recognizes the radical individuality of each person. When each one of us is born, his or her umbilical cord is cut, every one of us physically separated from mother, breathing on our own. Israel insists upon the independence of each person growing physically and emotionally, able to live in this world as a moral being.

In the presence of the divine, we have the potential to allow ourselves a full experience of our own particularity, our own individuality, without losing a sense of life's indivisibility. Conscious and unconscious, this recognition of the paradox of particularity and universality is a state of integrity in which we allow ourselves our own uniqueness, enabling us to meet each other with nothing between. Of course, ethnicity, race, and religion play important parts in our coming to an understanding of our particularity. Being in the presence of the divine, however, we know not to worship even the most personal parts of ourselves. We know, instead, to worship the source of the holy union of all humanity.

This experience of the worship of God, the worship of the spiritual source of our being, is a traditionally religious way for human beings to deal with the anxiety and fear inherent in being human. In our own time, we are seeing that there are other ways to experience the wonder of the wholeness of this feeling and thinking of integrity. There is no good reason for traditional religion to object to a proliferation of ways to such an experience. By the same reasoning, humanity would be foolish to turn its back on traditional paths, honed through hard human experience of the ages.

This is a moment in the history of *homo sapiens* when we need to rise above the limitations of old blinders so that we can continue to survive and grow. As technology tightens the connections amongst us, even as we are ever more shaken by the power of our weapons, we need to resist the temptation to think our fears can be stilled from without. Humanity's fears cannot be stilled through manipulation, particularly the toying with ethnic, racial, or religious loyalties.

Whatever the language of our spiritual beliefs and practices, we need to recognize that the primary goal of all human culture now must be to harness our arrogance and nurture our humility and obedience. We cannot understand ourselves without factoring in ethnicity, race, and religion, and we cannot continue to grow as a species without recognizing how we have to transcend the boundaries of such cultural categorization.

Religious Pluralism for Israel

Religious pluralism for Jews requires not only an acceptance that there are ways, other than *Torah*, through which to understand God's teaching, but also an understanding of *Torah* that thoroughly transcends ethnicity, race, and even religion. Before the God of Israel, we are all utterly naked. Every last bit of our cultural clothing is a projection of our nervous energy seeking air to breathe and trying to find solid ground upon which to stand.

It is human to delight in forms of cultural expression as personal as those of ethnicity, race, and religion. But the line is thin between meditating healthfully on one's particularity and being self-absorbed to the point of self-worship. If one chooses to speak a theological language, one must listen carefully to the ways that God's love commands humility.

When the spiritual tradition of Israel is not centered on the radical obedience of monotheism, it quickly loses its power to speak its own truth. There is a tension between dependence solely on God and any number of idolatrous memories. Even in First Temple times, there were carved idols within the Holy Temple. It is impossible to rely solely on God. Radical monotheism is an ideal; there are always ways that it is compromised. As we have seen, the spirit tends to become empty of itself; any expression of culture tends to objectify the personal. The goal always is the consciousness taught by the central prayer of Israel: *Hear O Israel, the Eternal One our God is One.*

Monotheistic religious traditions now must recognize the paradox that, though there are many ways of relating to divine truth, from the perspective of each tradition, there is only one way: uncompromising devotion to the source of all of what one holds holy, defined in its own particular way. To live through this paradox is difficult and requires much practice. We tend to underestimate the numbers of people already doing this spiritual practice, traditionally and non-traditionally.

In the twenty-first century, ethnicity, race, and religion increasingly will mingle. More and more people walking different spiritual paths will fall in love with each other and struggle to figure out how to ground their children in devotion to the source of all they hold sacred. The traditional spiritual traditions must open themselves to this reality, even as they also must insist on not compromising their own ways of teaching the radical integrity of humanity and the universe as a whole.

Reconstructing Israel

The ancient rabbis created a liturgy for the synagogue that is woven of the radical confidence in God that is warp and woof of *Hebrew Scriptures*: "Some trust in chariots and some in horses, but we will remember the name of the Eternal One our God." *(Psalm 20:8)* "Blessed is the one who trusts in the Eternal One." *(Jeremiah 17:7)* Such are the words of Psalmist and prophet that define the prayers of the *siddur* (traditional prayer book).

The message was no better received in Jeremiah's time than in our own. Around 600 b.c.e., the people of the southern kingdom of Judea remembered the Assyrians overrunning the homes of their sisters and brothers in the northern kingdom of Israel in 722 b.c.e.. When the Babylonians defeated the Assyrians and were about to conquer Judea, Jeremiah's trust in God did not appear to his neighbors to be sound advice. The prophet was despised by many of his people, some of whom wanted him dead. Jeremiah was not a pacifist, nor was he without courage in the face of an attacking enemy. He counseled going into exile because that was the word he heard from God.

Trusting in God is not an alternative to defending oneself physically when one can. It was trust in God that enabled Martin Buber to respond to Gandhi in the way that he did. In many of his psalms, King David sang of faith in the divine, even as he engaged in military battle. That Israel must physically defend itself is a given for anyone who truly is concerned about the well-being of Jews. Physical strength is necessary for Israel to survive physically in this world.

The modern nation-state of Israel came into existence out of the massive violence of the twentieth century. For Jews living in the Middle East, the reality of such violence never ceased. Given the power of weapons today, physical strength may be necessary for survival, but it also carries risks to everyone's survival. As noted above, we live at what appears to be a decisive turning point in human history. Simply put, given the power of our weapons today, we not only can mass murder each other; we can degrade the environment to a level low enough to call into question the survival of our species.

Say what you want about Israel's chosenness, the historical record is clear: the unfolding of human history often has involved the Jews, and there is a strange twist today as history unfolds. Despite the fact that the people of Israel were the victims of attempted genocide, many people in the world now point to the State of Israel as the major obstacle to peace. This is no accident. For two thousand years, Jews were contemptuously signaled out as particularly violent, responsible for Jesus' death and the murder of Christian children.

It is necessary in our time for humanity to disarm, but the world holds onto an old habit of blaming Jews if it believes that such disarmament begins with the people of Israel who were disarmed for two thousand years. The security of Jews world-wide depends upon the arsenal of the State of Israel. At the same time, the people of Israel long have known the moral equivalent of war. Even as they now refuse to contin-

ue to be bullied, they yearn for ways to sit down with those who fear
and hate them, to work through everybody's memories of hurt, so that
human life may persist on Earth.

Physical strength is necessary for Israel to survive in this world, but
it is not sufficient. Without its trust in God, Israel is not Israel. It is not
that, to be a Jew, one must "believe in God." Over the past few hundred years, many Jews have rejected theological explanations without
ceasing to be Jews, whatever their rabbis may have held. They continued to tell the old stories of the people of Israel. They insisted on understanding their own lives in the context of these stories, extracting from
them the means to live graciously in the pursuit of freedom. They were
who they were as a consequence of their clinging to the dreams and values of Israel.

Israel's faith, its trust in its God, is wounded today. The open-heart-
ed gratitude that was commanded by both the religion of ancient Israel
and rabbinical Judaism was scorched by the Nazis' partial success at
genocide. Gratitude still dwells in Israel's soul, but its heart was seared
by bitterness, a natural response to what Israel experienced. All through
its journey, Israel has known how tough love can be. Israel's trust in
God is its traditional way of responding to the toughness of this love.

Such unconditional love is a terrible struggle when we human
beings forget that we are not the source of our own existence; when we
think that we are or ought to be, or need to be in control. Nonetheless,
this love is the stuff of the cohesiveness of Israel, as of humanity as a
whole. Traditionally celebrated by Jews as *ahavat Yisrael* (the love of
Israel), this love cannot be understood without recognizing its spiritual
source. Whether or not the language of the people of Israel is theological, Israel cannot be understood merely as a people covenanted with
each other. *Ahavat Yisrael* is founded in the light of Israel, which is not
its own creation. This light is spiritual. Being Israel means being spiritual.

Of course, every people is spiritual and unique. Yet we do not lift
up the spirituality and uniqueness of humanity by denying Israel its
spiritual calling. Have we not learned that denial of the spirituality and
uniqueness of Israel leads to denial of human spirituality and uniqueness? The idea that Israel is a unique and spiritual nation is not only
compatible with our hopes for equality; it is a crucial ingredient in
humanity's quest to be free. Each of us is equal and unique, including
Israel. As goes Israel, so humanity may go, and perhaps Earth as well.

The existence of each human being and every human culture

depends upon a base line of self respect that comes with knowing one's own differences as both true and beautiful. The people of Israel are like all human beings. They need cultural boundaries within which to define themselves. Yet they cannot expect that they themselves alone will set the boundaries. The kind of order that allows for human growth comes from the inside out. What happens inside is a spiritual process, created as much if not more by the mystery of the workings of one's spiritual source than by any choices of one's own.

The challenge is to understand these processes of growth within the context of real, human culture. The culture of Israel is a laboratory within which human beings have experimented for thousands of years. The cutting edge of the spirituality and uniqueness of each Jew meets existing forms of Israel's culture in different ways for each person. Every Jew has his or her own perspective on where and how this meeting takes place. For some, the claims of personal growth are accorded more weight than existing forms of the tradition. For others, the established organization and institution are primary. There is no one correct way to be a Jew. There are shared meeting grounds, the variety of the streams of the tradition.

At this point, beyond recognizing that there is no one way to be a Jew, what is needed is the dedicated effort of many people, in many different kinds of communities, to shape the tradition through lives lived as Jews. Over time, if the past is any guide, we can expect to see the distilling out of spiritual ways which are shared by large numbers of Jews. This was the process through which rabbinical Judaism emerged from the religion of ancient Israel.

In 70 c.e., with the destruction of the Temple and the loss of sovereignty, the ancient rabbis took refuge in the idea of shaping the norms and values of Israel through engagement with sacred texts. More Jews now than ever before are learning in this way. The pre-modern, non-lineal genius of rabbinics survived modernity. The sages of Israel were correct in recognizing that there is no end to *talmud Torah*, the study of God's teaching.

Much of the impetus for the great interest in text study has come from the Orthodox world, but not all of it. The Reform, Conservative, and Reconstructionist streams of Judaism have educated many Jews in the study skills of *talmud Torah*. And many of those who have availed themselves of Orthodox teaching have rejected the authority of rabbis to define their observance of Judaism. They cherish the world-view of traditional texts; it fuels their personal growth. They appreciate the wisdom of Israel's sages. But they insist on the primacy of their own conscience.

Intermarriage

"Inamerica," a rabbi recently told his congregation, "the walls of discrimination have come tumbling down, and our future existence is imperiled precisely by the fulfillment of our fondest dream: living in a society where Jews don't have to be different." Indeed, the majority of marriages involving Jews in the United States now include a non-Jewish partner in the relationship. But it is not because Jews don't want to be different.

The fondest dream of Jews *is* to be different; to embrace difference as normal. There is a creative tension to the identity of Israel. Israel is called to resist human cruelty. Given the state of human affairs, from the time of Abraham and Sarah to the present, not conforming to humanity's viciousness leaves one vulnerable to its weakness. Israel is called to be different in ways that teach humanity to follow suit, everyone, equally different, together.

The great rise in the incidence of intermarriage amongst Jews in the Diaspora today cannot be attributed to a desire to be the same. The motivation behind intermarriage is complex and varied. Not the least cause of a Jew choosing a partner who is not a Jew is the actualization of the love that is at the core of Israel's values. In fact, as ethnic loyalties fade and the larger culture becomes increasingly homogenized, many Jews who are intermarrying continue to delight in the distinctiveness of Judaism. Given the opportunity in synagogue, week after week, they speak eloquently of their identity at the *b'nai mitzvah* of their spouses who have converted, and of their children.

Their problem is not that they are running away from who they are, ethnically or spiritually. They believed what they were taught at home and in synagogue about Israel's focus on freedom. With or without a relationship with God, they internalized the unconditional love of this relationship, and allowed this love to carry them to wherever it flowed. The essence of their life choices is more often a reflection of the teaching of Israel to reflect loving kindness in all relationship than it is a flight from being who they are. Their problem is the inability of the community of Israel to honor their personal experience. Religious or secular, they are taught the boundlessness of love. Then, when they fall in love, they are told that the community is sorry; this love, their love, it cannot affirm.

While some Jews still are embarrassed when love transcends race, the community would be ashamed to be caught shunning lovers who cross racial divides. At least intellectually, more and more Jews know that racial intermarriage is human destiny. But when it comes to religious intermarriage, leaders of the community, shuddering at the thought of a loss of continuity, leave the intermarried out in the cold, then condemn them for not coming inside. Where does the unconditional love go?

It is human to want our children to believe and identify as we do. For Jews after the Holocaust, there is a deeply internalized sense of responsibility not to break the chain. It is reasonable to be fearful about survival, to worry about the continuity of the peoplehood of Israel. Still, the problem faced by Israel is not intermarriage. It is that the people of Israel know so little about who Israel is. Jews want children to believe and identify as they do, even as they themselves are unclear about the identity of Israel. At a time when Israel itself has the means of worldly power, the temptation is to make an idol of the peoplehood of Israel; in effect, to keep the eyes of Israel closed to the spiritual light which calls Jews to be a people.

Humanity now looks about for such light. The historic religious traditions, amongst them Judaism, are treasures of wisdom for human beings emerging, broken and forlorn, from their love affair with modernity. What better time for the people of Israel to rediscover the power of the truth of its historic call to be a light unto the nations. Instead of worrying about boundaries, Israel needs to remember the power of its own truth.

The truth of Israel is neither intermarriage nor endogamy. The truth of Israel is the limitlessness and timelessness of God's promise to be Israel's partner. This is Israel's way of teaching about the truth of humanity as a whole. Israel's task is to be hospitable and grateful enough to remain personally open to respecting this love. Israel is not alone in this regard. Each of the historic faith traditions now is challenged to nurture persons whose deeds have direct relationship to their creeds.

We have to take ourselves seriously as religious citizens of democracy, seriously enough to bring the wisdom of historic religious traditions to the public square; not so seriously that any religion or even religion as a whole has a corner on the truth. Imagine the effect of millions of people consciously living out their creeds, remembering to put the love at the core of who they are before the interests of their own religious organizations. The sense of duty of which Chaim Nahman Bialik wrote would begin to emerge.

Embracing pluralism is not the acceptance of the least common denominator. Pluralism nurtures attitudes of the soul that are essential to the fulfillment of the promises of democracy. To be democratic is to be pluralistic. Human beings will not stop killing each other without the acceptance of pluralism. There are reasons why pluralism is hated, disparaged, and feared by those who insist that theirs is the only way to live. Theirs may well be a road to human freedom, but only inasmuch as they relinquish the idea that it is the only road.

As the human capacity to kill grows exponentially, the feminist idea that the personal is political suggests that the spiritual is political as well. Not that organized religion becomes involved in politics. Rather, that what we call politics be infused with the imperatives of the spirit.

The Psalmist says, "The Eternal One is our light and our salvation, the source of real strength." *(Psalm 27:1)* If we human beings truly want to, we can free ourselves of war, injustice and hatred. After the twentieth century, many of us already have begun to see that there is no salvation in guns and money. After September 11th, each one of us must pledge to challenge the arrogance, the assumptions of superiority, found anywhere in our own religion.

For Jews in the Diaspora, the challenge is to accept intermarriage as a natural development of humanity in the twenty-first century. For people of Israel, the time has come to reconsider who is a Jew. Maybe what is emerging now is a return to a more existential way of understanding Israel. Israel exists in the way the people of Israel live. How Israel lived in the past is significant in shaping the transmission of Jewish identity, but not as important as Jews living as members of the people of Israel in the present.

Two thousand years ago, Israel survived the end of the sacrificial cult of the Temple through the transforming genius of the rabbis. Now it is time for Israel to change again, this time shedding the skin of ethnicity as a determinant of its identity. The leadership of Israel defies reality when it confers the status of Judaism on one, born of a Jewish mother (or father) who knows nothing about Israel and makes no effort to learn and teach; while denying membership in Israel to one who is not considered to be a Jew under the old *halakhah*, though he or she is educated as a Jew, decides right from wrong as a Jew, and lives by the calendar of Israel. Ethnicity, for thousands of years a protector of Israel's survival, may have exhausted its usefulness in the unfolding of the mystery of Israel.

The transmission of the calling of the people of Israel is a process that can be studied, but not fully understood. The unfolding of Israel's story is a mystery whose secrets only very slowly are revealed, if they are revealed at all. It would be better for Israel to return to worship of the source of this mystery than to bow down at the altar of self pride.

Non-lineal Israel

Throughout the history of Israel, the identity of parents was a key part of a person's identity. If you were born to Israelites, you were an Israelite. The issue revolved around the identity of your father in biblical times and of your mother in rabbinical times. Family was and remained the primary teacher of Israel's identity.

In its essence, however, Israel is called beyond lineality. Israel is a spiritual nation, and the spirit defies lineage. Moses must be free to sit and listen in Rabbi Akiba's classroom. Elijah must be present at every Passover *seder* and *brit milah* (ritual circumcision). *Talmud Torah*, the learning of the ancient rabbis, is not lineal.

Israel certainly knows the harsh realities of time. The children of Israel were exiled from the land of Israel in time. The Allies failed to bomb the railroad tracks to Auschwitz in time. Israel still is not able to pray in peace in Jerusalem. The words of Israel's prophets insist on justice in time.

Israel is humanity wrestling with its demons in time. Yet, what has enabled Israel to persevere is its knowledge of the spiritual flow of the universe that is beyond time. The people of Israel now are called to reaffirm this spiritual understanding, even as, out of their own painful experience, they sound the alarm for humanity, warning *homo sapiens* that, as a species, we are at the edge of oblivion.

The threats to Israel and to humanity are the same. When humanity considers the prospects of a universe without human beings, Israel's knowledge of the unconditional spiritual flow of God is challenged. The myth of Israel is a story of an extended family of human beings struggling to remember that their opportunity to live freely on Earth depends upon their recognition that there is a source of life that transcends material existence; and that humanity is responsible for living in this light.

As a spiritual people, Israel knows the bankruptcy of international competition; the folly of one nation thinking itself superior to another. Two thousand years ago, the ancient rabbis taught that "just a single person was created in the beginning so that no one could say to another: 'My father was greater than your father.'" The only true lineage of humanity is its connection to the spiritual source of its existence. The ancient Hebrew word for clan, *mishpahah*, is related to the idea of pouring, effusion. Israel's understanding of family transcends the transmission of blood, of genes. The family of Israel is fed by the effusion of the spirit, the flow of the divine through life.

The name of a child of Israel is a composite of a given name and parents' names. For example, a male is called *Yitzhak ben Avraham v'Sarah* (Isaac son of Abraham and Sarah); a female, *Dinah bat Yaakov v'Leah* (Dinah daughter of Jacob and Leah). All converts to Judaism traditionally take the parental names of Abraham and Sarah. The idea is that, when one becomes a Jew, one inherits the seed of Israel, going back to the first Israelites, Abraham and Sarah. The fact that Judaism historically has had mixed feelings about converts perhaps accounts for the tradition of signaling out converts as son or daughter of *Avraham avinu v'Sarah imanu* (Abraham our father and Sarah our mother). It is a practice rejected by many rabbis today, who prefer the understanding that a Jew is a Jew, regardless of how he or she came to be a Jew.

As we have seen, already a thousand years ago, Maimonides understood this seed to be a spiritual inheritance rather than a matter of biology. What is the substance of this spirituality if not the historic teaching that Israel's is a story of an extended family of human beings struggling to remember that their opportunity to live freely on Earth depends upon their recognition that there is a source of life which transcends material existence. The uncompromising optimism of this teaching is the essence of the synagogue liturgy created by the ancient rabbis. As ever, the fate of Israel depends upon its grasping and teaching the hope of this unconditionality of God's love for Israel (humanity).

The spirit is tough. The Psalmist says, "For God's loving kindness endures forever." (Psalm 118:1). The spirit is tough enough to exist for eternity. Human freedom is predicated on this hope. Life is a fire unconsumed.

"Everything is foreseen," Rabbi Akiba taught, "and free choice is given." The primary danger for the people of Israel is thinking that their survival is in their own hands. Israel would then make the mistake which threatens humanity as a whole. In a world in which *The Secrets of the Protocols of Zion* continues to circulate, Israel has cause for concern about threats from without. But the greatest threat always is Israel's forgetting its own spiritual source.

Just as human arrogance threatens to break the bonds of the covenant between human beings and God, the people of Israel need to rediscover the depths of their historic gratitude for being, so that they, once again, are able to share the gift of eternity inherent in knowing the unconditionality of the spirit. Instead of worrying about the parameters of its peoplehood, Israel needs to be focused on the fire at its core.

Israel recognizes the wellspring of humanity through its experience of telling and retelling the stories of Israel's redemption by God. The return of the people of Israel to the land promised to Abraham and Sarah was epochal, and it is dangerous to underestimate its value. But there is a limit to what Israel can learn from reestablishing itself on its historic land. Martin Luther King, Jr., who loved the story of Israel, reminded all of us that "(s)alvation is being on the right road, not having a destination." At no time in its history more than now, Israel is realizing that its journey does not end with a return to Canaan. As long as Israel breathes, there is the task to discover the right road, and find it over and over again.

The Jews of the State of Israel teach the world that Judaism is not about victimhood. This lesson goes deeper even than the self respect of self defense. All over the world, the people of Israel need to breathe in and out the air of freedom. Before the death of the last survivor of the camps, however, the people of Israel owe to all who suffered, particularly to the memory of those who perished, a radical regeneration of the gratitude that grows naturally at Israel's heart.

Torah reports that when the matriarch Leah gave birth to her fourth son, she named him *Yehudah* (Judah), from the Hebrew root meaning "to praise." In Hebrew, a Jew is *yehudi*, one who is grateful.

Reclaiming the Yoke

Reclaiming the Yoke

I srael is Israel when its people cherish responding to God's command. To be Israel, Israel must be willing to bear the yoke of *mitzvah* (commandment). As we have seen, the concept of *mitzvah* predates the rabbis' definition of *mitzvah*. Abraham and Sarah bore the yoke of *mitzvah* by accepting the experience of living unconditionally. Moses and the children of Israel accepted this responsibility. Though often reluctant, the prophets of Israel embraced *mitzvah*.

When bearing the yoke, there is no inclination to exchange tit for tat; no projecting one's own fears onto another. Cherishing God's *mitzvah*, one responds like Abraham, going for oneself as one goes to oneself, and going to oneself as one goes for oneself. This is the foundation of the freedom of Israel.

It would be difficult to wear the yoke, even for a short time, without laughing and crying, knowing joy and despair. Accepting the sovereignty of God often requires patience. It always creates patience. Sometime it asks for a stilling of anger. More often, it creates a vent for anger, so that justice may prevail. Strangely enough, the more one freely clings to this sense of obedience, the greater one's freedom. In words of a song that we teach our children, "love isn't love until we give it away."

The anti-Semitic notion of the controlling Jew is a misrepresentation of the opposite: Israel's call to abandon itself to service of the spiritual source of its being. It is no different for every human being. We are all confounded by Rabbi Akiba's paradox that everything is foreseen and free choice is given. Without an appreciation of this paradox, we over-react and under-react; try too hard and do not do enough. In this futility, we demonstrate a lack of respect for our own lives. We would be better served to accept *mitzvah* as the way for us, truly, to be free.

There is a limit to how much disrespect for life *homo sapiens* can show and continue to survive. There is a connection between our capacity to accept the demands of our conscience and our self respect. The greater our recognition that we are commanded by the source of our being, the more that we care for who we are in being human. As ever, the vast majority of humanity shares a longing for a healthy sense of responsibility, whether it is understood in religious language of being commanded by God or in secular terms of acting in the world in accord with one's own conscience.

Either way, for those who are focused on living righteously without

insisting that everyone else live in the same way, the central commandment is to accept and experience ourselves as the persons who we truly
are. Each of us is charged with being able to say, with conviction that
"the world was created for my sake, no less and no more than it was created for yours." One can gauge the measure of one's own integrity by
the extent to which one has the courage to recognize that one's challenge is to accept the equality of everyone's uniqueness, beginning with
one's own.

ACKNOWLEDGEMENTS

This book is more a work of *midrash* than of history. Trained both as an historian and a rabbi, I am mindful of the difference and sensitive to the standards of documentation of each discipline. There are no footnotes here. Where I have quoted directly, I have endeavored to identify the source. I have not hesitated to weave my own midrashic understanding within my recounting of biblical and rabbinic stories.

Much of the material presented here first took form as parts of sermons for which sources were not noted at the time. English translations of Hebrew texts are a combination of my own and those of others, and sometimes I have combined the two. I am grateful for Ellen Frankel's work, both for particular stories in *The Classical Tales*, and for her example of midrashic freedom generally.

I came to The Jewish Theological Seminary as a *tabula rasa* with regard to rabbinics. I thank my teachers for their patience and devotion. Clearly, the central ideas of this book fall outside the pale of current thinking amongst leaders of Conservative Judaism. I do remember one of my teachers (a Conservative rabbi) asking: "Who were the rabbis to place themselves between God and the Jewish people?" I alone, of course, am responsible for the ideas presented here.

I have learned much from members of Ohavi Zedek Synagogue, too many to name. I thank all the members of the synagogue for affording me a three month sabbatical during which much of this book was written. Special thanks to Ruth Horowitz and Luis Manuel Oropeza for their helpful criticism. I am grateful to Gary Visco, Robert Kaplan and Milt Potash and his family for their generosity. Much thanks to Steve Alexander for his design wisdom and good nature. I am grateful to Mardie Luppold for permission to reproduce her artwork on the book jacket.

My mother and father, Evelyn and William Chasan, grounded me in a love of a Judaism that defied Jewish religion. I hope to describe elsewhere my journey from secular to religious identity.

I am grateful beyond words to my family, Kathy, Cavan, Zev and Ari whose love has helped me to hold onto my dreams.

This book is dedicated to my father-in-law, Ray Comstock, in whose home it was written, and from whose dignity and grace I learn each day.

Index of Biblical Passages

General Index